PUAKŌ

An Affectionate History

To Charlene Mary Morrison for the Puakō Historical Society

The life story of a small community

on the South Kohala Coast

of the Island of Hawai'i

Researched, compiled and written

by the Puakō Historical Society

2000

Canadian Cataloguing in Publication Data

Puakō : an affectionate history : the life story
of a small community on the South Kohala coast
of the island of Hawaii

Includes bibliographical references.
ISBN 1-894694-00-7

1. Puakō (Hawaii)--History.
I. Puakō Historical Society.
DU629.P82P82 2000   996.9'1   C00-901201-X

Book Design: Fiona Raven
Proofreader: Neall Calvert

First printing September 2000

Creative Connections Publishing

Suite 212 - 1656 Duranleau Street • Granville Island
• Vancouver, B.C. V6H 3S4 • 604-688-0320 •
email: ccpublishing@axion.net
www.creativeconnectionspublishing.com

Affiliated Publishers in
Vancouver • Calgary • Milwaukee • Denver

Printed in Hong Kong

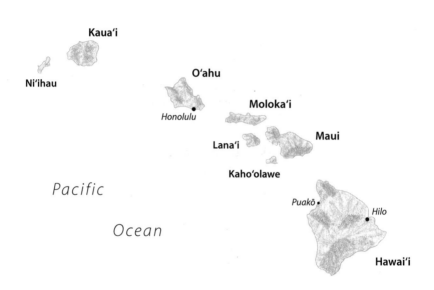

Kaua'i

Ni'ihau

O'ahu

Honolulu

Moloka'i

Lana'i

Maui

Kaho'olawe

Pacific

Ocean

Puakō

Hilo

Hawai'i

The Hawaiian Islands

TABLE OF CONTENTS

PREFACE

This book had its beginnings in 1990 when a few residents of Puakō gathered together to form the Puakō Historical Society, a committee of the Puakō Community Association. We were concerned that, as the older generation moved on (one way or another), a great many memories were being lost; and beyond that there had never been any organized effort to document the entire span of human habitation in this bit of shoreline on the Kohala Coast. We decided to research, compile and write a local history of Puakō, dedicating any profits from the book to the preservation of this heritage. Ten years later, we have achieved the first part of our goal.

Our resident committee members were Audrey Whittall (Chair), John Hoover, Katy Lowrey, Mary Morrison (Writer), Helen Pickering, and Marcia Sammons and Susan Schulze (both now deceased). Although technically not a Puakō inhabitant, John Hoover, Rector of the Hōkūloa Church, qualified as one of the most active members of our community.

And Sandy Ednie, of Waimea, was an interested visitor to some meetings.

Our first activity was to order large quantities of stationery, most of which is still sitting in a box somewhere. Then we began the long, slow process of accumulating information. We tracked down out-of-print books and other publications; we conducted interviews (sometimes of each other), reviewed oral histories, delved into land records, borrowed family photographs and plumbed the depths of library and museum stacks. Our goal, wherever possible, was to use primary sources and/ or museum-based research. Much of the process was a long, uphill slog, but there were also euphoric moments of serendipity. Two of the best were the discovery of Mary Austin's handwritten copies, from the Library of Congress, of explorers' journals pertaining to this coast and the gift of material from the personal diaries of Ichiro Goto, a fascinated and fascinating observer of Puakō in the first half of the twentieth century.

In the course of the research and the writing, we have found much to cherish in this little community. It gives us great joy to share it with you.

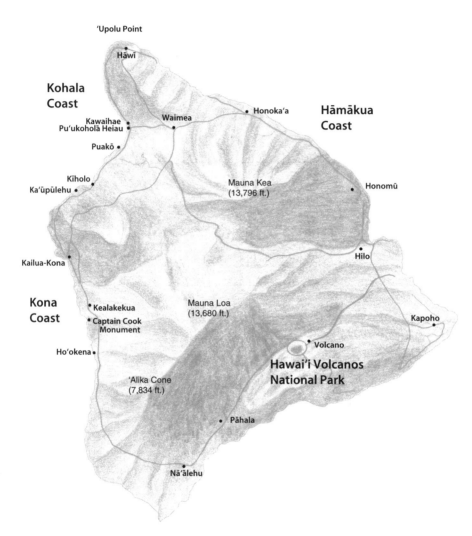

Hawai'i, The Big Island

ACKNOWLEDGEMENTS

Although Puakō is about a place, it is a place shaped by people. In this regard, our research and writing was much the same: People got us off and running; people shared their memories, their family photographs, their scientific knowledge, even, sometimes, their passions and their pocketbooks. We must begin our thanks with some of these individuals.

We are grateful to Rick Schulze, who was President of the Puakō Community Association when this project was sanctioned, and to all the succeeding presidents and boards that have supported us.

Local residents, both present and past, have given us vital written and oral history. Papa Henry Auwae shared remembrances of his family and a mother lode of local lore. We received input from members of the Akau and Doi families, longtime inhabitants of the Kawaihae area. We are grateful to Alan White, an early resident, for his productive interview. Bill and Jan Adams shared their painting of the Akona house with us. Annie Martinson, granddaughter of Annie Laau and step-granddaughter of Jack Paulo, was kind enough to answer many questions in connection with her family history, as was Momi Shoemaker, the daughter of "Buck" Puakea. Mrs. Fujii, who still lives in Puakō, gave us information on her husband, Bunji, who ran the charcoal operation in Puakō for many years. Andy Morgan and Herbert De Luz told us their family stories about the land auction.

Long-time residents Leon Thevenin and Ed Austin shared valuable writings and answered our many questions with great patience. Mary Austin offered us the use of her remarkable copies of the explorers' journals. Tita Ruddle Spielman generously provided us with family photographs of the early days in Puakō. Don and Diane Hause loaned us their portrait of Kamehameha, and Robert Lyn Nelson Studio gave us permission to reproduce it. Katy Wishard Lowrey shared with the other committee members a whole treasure chest of memories and associations from 1929 to the present. Particularly, we are grateful to Tom Goto, whose parents and grandparents lived in Puakō from 1902 to 1997. He granted us access to his father's notes and journals and to family photographs that could have been a book in themselves.

From outside Puakō, we are indebted to the late

Dick Penhallow for information on the wells, Ian Birnie for the history of the railroad that served the sugar mill and James Murray of Murray, Smith & Co., who provided information about his father, the surveyor of the Puakō Beach lots in 1950. Thanks also to Ski Kwiatkowski and Emmett Cahill for invaluable suggestions on publishing. And we owe a very special debt of gratitude to Bob Gibson, former Foreign Editor of the *Los Angeles Times*, who, out of the goodness of a very large heart, made us a gift of his considerable professional skills as an editor.

Institutions gave us aid and assistance in so many ways. The Bishop Museum in Honolulu was a bastion of support, and we are grateful to them for permission to print photographs from their collection. From out-of-print books through Hawaiian spellings and archival advice, they were there for us—in particular Desoto Brown and Ron Schaeffer in the Archives Department and Patrice Belcher in the Library. The Honolulu Academy of Arts was helpful in allowing us to reprint a photograph of the Emmert watercolor of Puakō. Both the Lyman House Memorial Museum in Hilo and the Kona Historical Society in Kailua-Kona have been invaluable resources for information and photographs. The Hawaii Agricultural Research Center provided production figures for the Puakō plantation, and Robert H. Hughes of the Hawaiian Sugar Planters' Association showed us where to look for information on the sugar-mill operation. Yvonne Nelson of Title Guaranty of Hawaii, Inc. helped us with research on land records. The management and staff of the Mauna Lani Resort, particularly the late Francine Duncan, shared valuable material pertaining to the history of Kalāhuipua'a and Francis I'i Brown. A former Mauna Lani Resort staff member, Leilani Hino, assisted the committee with everything from logo design to archeological data.

Through the offices of the Rev. John Hoover, we obtained access to and permission to use excerpts from Lorenzo Lyons' annual *Waimea Reports*, now the property of the Hawaiian Mission Children's Society Library. We also are grateful to *West Hawaii Today* for allowing us to use Leilani Hino's material on the Puakō fire and to *Narrow Gauge and Shortline Gazette* and Malcolm Gaddis for the picture of the locomotive in the Dillingham quarry.

Last, but not least, our profound thanks to the small group of stalwarts who quietly put up the money to make the publication of this book possible.

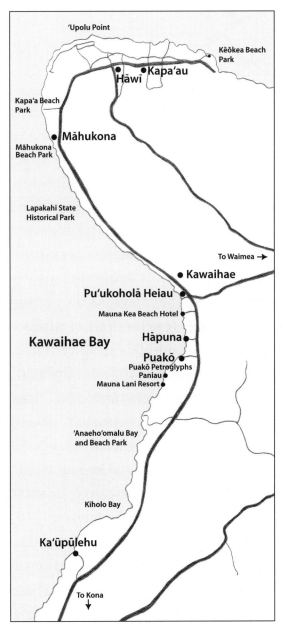

'Upolu Point

Kēōkea Beach Park

Kapa'au
Hāwī

Kapa'a Beach Park

Māhukona

Māhukona Beach Park

Lapakahi State Historical Park

To Waimea →

Kawaihae

Pu'ukoholā Heiau

Mauna Kea Beach Hotel

Kawaihae Bay

Hāpuna

Puakō
Puakō Petroglyphs
Paniau
Mauna Lani Resort

'Anaeho'omalu Bay and Beach Park

Kīholo Bay

Ka'ūpūlehu

To Kona
↓

Kohala Coast, Hawai'i, The Big Island

 INTRODUCTION

When we walk along the road in Puakō, we tread, in part, along pathways almost a thousand years old. In ancient times, these paths were marked on the lava with bits of coral, and they were worn into the pili grass and the sandy soil by the feet of ancient Polynesian people who had come here for some of the same reasons we have. They came because they thought they could make a living, and if the results did not always meet their expectations, some of them stayed on anyhow. There has never been a time in the history of Puakō when all the settlers moved on. Something has kept people here in continuous residence for almost a millennium—some trick of coastal beauty that enchants the senses, some feeling of place that lifts the heart at the first glimpse of the startlingly blue water and the embracing bays.

We stand along the beach at sunset and wait for the evening colors to come up, just as they did. We feel the night air like warm water on our skin, and they must have felt the same sensation. Our children learn to swim in the same pools theirs used.

We share the same squid holes; we spear the same fish. We have a tradition here of loving care for this little place, and it has been handed down from them.

There are those who say some of the ancient Hawaiians are still here. From time to time there have been reports of sounds in the night—marching noises, walking noises, soft Hawaiian voices calling back and forth. In 1952, Richard Smart, the late owner of the Parker Ranch, built a house in Puakō that he slept in only once. In the morning he announced warriors had been going through his bedroom all night; he packed up hastily and never returned. It is perhaps interesting that an archeological dig near the site of that house had turned up fish hooks and cooking implements but no weapons of war.

Nothing that the outside world would regard as really important has ever happened here, and no one terribly important to the world has ever lived here, but the winds of history have blown through Puakō like an ʻŌlauniu gale. All of the people who have lived here have been influenced by its gusts, and there is a good, rich story to tell about these men and women who were our neighbors.

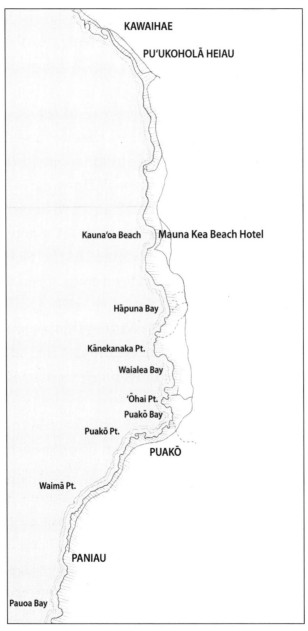

KAWAIHAE

PU'UKOHOLĀ HEIAU

Kauna'oa Beach   Mauna Kea Beach Hotel

Hāpuna Bay

Kānekanaka Pt.

Waialea Bay

'Ōhai Pt.

Puakō Bay

Puakō Pt.

PUAKŌ

Waimā Pt.

PANIAU

Pauoa Bay

Detail of Puakō area

Chapter I

THE FIRST
TO ARRIVE

Long, dangerous ocean voyage
A fishing, not farming, community
A legendary appetite for octopus

Our little settlement of Puakō Beach today
fronts a single road on the Big Island that starts
at the Queen Ka'ahumanu Highway, ambles along
the shoreline for three miles and terminates at
Paniau, until recently the Ruddle Estate. It lies
south of Hāpuna Beach State Park and Waialea
Bay and just north of Mauna Lani Resort, the
old ahupua'a, or Hawaiian land division, of
Kalāhuipua'a. The major portion of Puakō land,
in the ahupua'a of Lalamilo, was subdivided by the
Territory of Hawai'i in the early 1950s into approxi-
mately one hundred and sixty lots. They were sold
at auction with the proviso that a building cost-
ing at least one thousand dollars be constructed

on the property within five years. Many of those houses still stand today, and they are the basis of the contemporary Puakō. But the real roots of Puakō lie deep in Hawaiian history, and it is there that our story begins.

When family groups first came to the Kohala Coast between AD 750 and AD 1000, they were part of a Diaspora from the windward side of the island where the original Polynesian settlements had occurred sometime after the second century AD. These people had come from the islands of the Marquesas, almost three thousand miles to the south, on a long and perilous ocean voyage, probably as refugees from warfare there. They brought with them, in their great double sailing canoes, plants and domestic animals. Their most immediate need was a nurturing environment for agriculture, because they found only minimal indigenous foodstuff in Hawai'i. They lived on seafood and birds, ferns and berries until they could breed their pigs, raise their chickens and harvest their first crops. They sought the most fertile areas—the mouths of valleys on windward shores where streams brought down rich, red, volcanic earth from the mountains and where the rainfall would nourish their plants. In particular, they planted taro and sweet potatoes and their beloved coconut palms, and they moved from the seashore inland as they established their foothold on the land.

On the island of Hawai'i, they suckled at the breasts of the great eastern valleys as infant colonies, but as the settlements matured they were forced to move out to other areas. Because of the agrarian nature of their culture, these first Hawaiians lived in rather isolated environments. As in all subsistence farming, there could be no large settlements, for the raising of food crops preordained the individual farmer living in the midst of his fields. It also limited the number of people who could be supported on any given area of land, and by the latter part of the first millennium some of the colonists were beginning to fan out to the leeward side of the island. Exploring the coastline in their canoes, following and improving the shoreline trails and moving across the mountain saddles, they established the ahupua'a land divisions of the western territory, sometimes marking the boundaries with cairns. They found temporary shelter in lava tubes, and they made rough, walled structures to protect themselves and their families from the wind; and where they found a hospitable environment, they stayed, and permanent villages began to develop.

On the arid Kohala Coast, there was an entirely

different pattern of settlement than on the wind-ward shores. Livelihoods were based on fishing rather than the agriculture afforded by the fertile valleys of the other side of the island. Where there was a source of potable water, a harbor beach or a pass through the reef for canoes and an offshore fishery, whole groups of Hawaiians settled together. Such farming as could be developed was only marginal and dependent on diverting intermit-tently running streams into ʻauwai, or irrigation ditches, to enable them to grow minimal amounts of dry taro and sweet potatoes. In some cases the settlers were drawn to areas where there were no streams at all, because the fishing was better where silt did not wash into the ocean. Where con-ditions were particularly favorable, sizable fishing villages evolved. This was a form of colonization that favored aggregation, as opposed to the farm-ing communities that favored dispersal. This is the sort of habitation that happened here in Puakō.

The whole area from Kawaihae south to ʻAnaehoʻomalu had natural features that made it hospitable to fishermen and their families. At Kawaihae there was the most protected harbor of this section of the island and a source of water which was highly prized. The name Kawaihae means "water of the wrath of the people" and refers to the fights over a pond of potable water there. The bay of Hāpuna was named for a spring-fed pool there. A reef, which was largely destroyed by the tsunami of 1946, stretched from what is now Spencer Beach to Kalāhuipua'a and was awash at high tide. It provided both protection from the waves and a seaborn path along parts of the coast. In Puakō and Paniau, at that time, there were good canoe passes through the reef and wide, white sandy beaches. A freshwater spring formed a pool on the shore at Puakō near where the church is today, and there were several more springs at Kalāhuipua'a. The shoreline in those days was as much as three feet higher in places than it is to-day, and many of the springs that are in the ocean now were on dry land. The lava outcroppings on the beach and the low-lying rocky points in the Puakō area lent themselves to forming basins for the production of salt from sea water; the salt was used as a preservative for fish, as seasoning and as medicine. Just offshore, these same lava forma-tions supported a growth of limu, a seaweed that the Hawaiians were fond of eating.

One of the most exciting discoveries the original settlers made here were the anchialine ponds that stretched from Puakō south to 'Anaeho'omalu. Unique to this coast, these pools were formed by underground runoff from the upland area that was trapped near the shore. The ponds were not connected directly to the sea but had tidal action within them through porous rock and a series of lava tubes. Brackish but marginally potable, these waters were developed by the settlers into holding tanks for saltwater fish, mollusks and turtles.

These natural features were the attributes that made the Puakō area more congenial to settlers than many other portions of the coast, but it was not otherwise an inviting environment. At the north end of the Kīholo Lava Plain, the landscape was formed by a series of overlapping lava flows that were like drippings of candle wax. The lava from an ancient eruption of Mauna Kea and from an even older one of Mauna Loa had formed a broad delta area that invited occasional floods from the mountainside drainage, and the alluvial deposits from these floods had mixed with the wave-collected beach sand to form a sandy, infertile and frequently windblown soil. It was not a promising place for agriculture.

Very little grew naturally in this bleak landscape, and only the pili grass remains here today from pre-Hawaiian times. There were then a few other plants growing wild, mostly dwarfish cousins of the rainforest trees and shrubs found at higher elevations that had adapted to the arid soil. There was some lehua, kou and small varieties of both the 'iliahi and heau sandalwoods. A stubby, curly grained koa was found near the shore, and later it was prized for idol carving, but, for the moment, Puakō presented a forbidding vista, until the settlers looked to the water. There they found the compelling beauty of the shoreline and all the richness of the sea.

Where the lava from Mauna Loa entered the sea, a basalt shelf with numerous outcroppings had formed, with portions just under water at low tide. Meandering corals had been attracted to the relatively level surface, and the resulting growth had formed a secondary reef at Puakō that was unique on the leeward coast of the island. Toward the open sea there was a sharp vertical drop-off, forming an underwater cliff two hundred and fifty to seven hundred feet offshore that fronted a sandy bottom. This unusual configuration resulted in an ideal environment for a wide variety of reef fish, crustaceans and mollusks, particularly octopus. It also provided one of the major coastal habitats for green sea turtles, which rested in the caves on the cliff face, fed in the shallows on algae and seaweed, and basked on the rocks, as they still do at places along the shore today.

Here was food—a steady and plentiful supply
that could support whole villages of family groups.
Here was a little cove where canoes could be built
and launched. Here was water of one sort or another and salt and limu. A life could be made in
this place, and the shore could become an oasis to
complement the abundant resources of the sea.
Some of the straggling groups of Hawaiians that
had been traveling up and down the shore settled
and started to build a village, sometime between
900 and 1200 AD.

Legend has it that the settlement was the result
of the love story of the Princess Puakō and
Lālāmilo. Puakō (whose name meant either "the
tassel of the sugar cane" or Puakou, "the flower of
the Kou tree") and her sister, ʻAnaehoʻomalu, were
born in Puna and lived there until their inordinate
love of octopus and fish led their father to send
them out of the district to search for husbands to
provide for them. Puakō trudged north over the
lava trails until she reached Waimā, the point
midway down today's Puakō Beach Drive. There
she met a woman, Neʻula, whom she told of her
great love of heʻe, or octopus. Neʻula introduced her
to her son, Lālāmilo, who was renowned as a fisherman of the species. It was love at first meeting
when he compared Puakō to the finest heʻe he could

Cowrie Lure. Photograph. Bishop Museum.

catch. They married soon after, and things only got better. One day Puakō found such an enormous octopus on the reef that her husband could not believe she had caught it herself. On investigation they found another huge heʻe huddled in the same spot, over a hole that contained a large cowrie shell which glowed red like an ōhiʻa blossom. They pried the shell loose and incorporated it into a lure that became legendary when a hundred and twenty octopuses climbed into Lālāmilo's canoe in pursuit of the device.

The design became famous throughout the islands, and the site of the discovery of the shell and the broader region of the entire ahupuaʻa became known as Puakō. It was not until 1928 that the district became Lālāmilo and the settlement alone retained the ancient name.

Chapter II

SMALL-TOWN
POLYNESIAN
LIFE
1000 to 1779

Petroglyphs: news of the neighborhood
Grand warfare on Puakō's plains
The saltmaker's brief marriage
Tale of a thieving dog

Waimā Point, where Puakō and Lālāmilo lived,
was a saltmaking area, the name signifying the
changing color of the water as it evaporated. The
village itself evolved inland from Paniau (the
southernmost section of Puakō), about three-
quarters of a mile north of Pauoa Bay. It lay close
to a trail and far enough from the sea to provide a
measure of protection from marauders.

At first the families huddled in the lava tubes
and caves and built c-shaped walls that functioned
as temporary shelters from the wind. As time went

on, a more formal village evolved from several large kauhale, or extended family groups. The village center was a large mua, or eating-house. It was an imposing structure built on a heavy stone platform, and it functioned as a sort of men's club. There males of the village ate their meals, gathered to celebrate rituals such as the ceremonial drinking of kava and performed workshop duties such as the fabrication of tools and fishhooks.

The hales, or houses, of the community were built around this one-building downtown. Most were pili-roofed structures, some on stone foundations, others more like enclosures than buildings. Nearby the Hawaiians made rings of rock and piles of stones that probably served as burial sites. Some of these can be observed today. The lava tubes and caves were still used as tool-making sites and as tombs after they were abandoned as dwellings. One of the Paniau caves continued to be a site for interments into at least the latter part of the nineteenth century and is well-documented in archeological studies.

As the village matured, some of the Hawaiians began to move to the suburbs. There was at least one hale built on the shore behind the present location of the Hōkūloa Church, and many others were constructed along the beach during the pre-

European era. By 1800 the original village lay virtually abandoned and the major settlement was in the area between the present-day boat ramp and the Hōkūloa Church. Early written accounts by explorers and whalers mention seeing many signs of habitation from their ships. Another small group of houses was built on the hill near the present entry road to Puakō from the Queen Ka'ahumanu Highway. Several c-shaped shelters have been found there, together with two stone enclosures and some circular stone paving. Parts of these structures were recycled as cairns and grave markers in the early twentieth century when the same area was used as a small cemetery.

Another small grouping of houses and fishing trails could be seen on the bluff of Kānekanaka Point (then called Kanakanaka) at the northern edge of Waialea Bay, and there were scattered dwellings that appeared, over time, throughout the area of Hāpuna Bay.

When they built their hales, the Hawaiians planted trees and flowers among them, and the area became quite verdant. There were tall, graceful coconut palms along the shore, and a great many dwarf nuts, or loulus, as well. The settlers cultivated pandanus for the fibers, from which the women wove the lauhala mats for which Puakō

Woman weaving mat.

eventually became well known. Hau grew here and dropped its dark orange blossoms into the fishponds in the late afternoon. Breadfruit trees were rooted in the sandy soil and they gave their fruit for food, their bark for the manufacture of tapa and their sap for canoe caulking. Some dryland sweet potatoes and taro were grown, but the major vegetable farms favored sites toward the slopes of Mauna Kea, where there was better soil, more rain and streams for irrigation. Because these crops could not be tended on a daily basis from the village, some of the relatives moved out to establish satellite groups that were known by the same family names as their kin who remained at the shore. The farms there were noted for their sugar cane, bananas and 'awa (or kava), and the produce traveled to the shore along a series of downhill trails.

On the hill near the present road, the people of Puakō built the heiau Pahauna, which was a shrine to medicine. It was built not long after the settlement and restored by Kekuaokalani, the champion of traditional Hawaiian religious values, sometime shortly before his death in 1819. One sentinel stone from the restoration, an upright about six feet tall, was called Pelikane, or English-man, by Kekuaokalani. The big, shaped rock has disappeared, but a few of the building stones can still be seen on the site. This heiau was an impor-tant link in a chain of ancient shrines on this part of the coast. Kauhuhu Heiau, now under water, stood a quarter of a mile north of Puakō Point and was named for a minor deity, a shark god who lived in a cave on Moloka'i. Kapo, the care-giving heiau dedicated to the sorcery god, stood near the present Mauna Kea Beach Hotel. Mahikihia, a burial heiau, was in the same general area. There were

Mailekini and Hale-o-Kapuni, both near Spencer Beach Park, one onshore and the other a shark-feeding shrine in the water. And, in 1790, the grandest of them all was constructed by Kamehameha the Great, the forbidding Puʻukoholā that frowns at the entire coastline from its promontory above the much older Mailekini.

The most remarkable contribution that the settlers of Puakō made to the prehistory of this area, though, was the field of petroglyphs they created near the major settlement and alongside the Kaʻeo Trail. More than three thousand figures, pecked and incised into the lava in three enormous groups, constitute the finest petroglyph field in the Hawaiian Islands. They are among the oldest carvings found on the island, and the work went on for a longer continuous period than at any other site. Why here? Why would our struggling little fishing village devote itself, over centuries, to what would at first glance appear to be meaningless doodles in the lava? The answer lies in comparison with other petroglyph fields.

In the concentration near the trail at ʻAnaehoʻomalu on this same coast, for example, the oldest petroglyphs have no unifying force or theme. They are an excellent example of harmless graffiti executed at a spot where traveling Hawaiians stopped for water and sheltered in caves and lava tubes. In Puʻuloa, at the south end of the island, the petroglyph field began as piko holes, which were repositories for umbilical cords of the new-born, and eventually became non-literal family tallies of the various communal groups there. The plot in Puakō began in a similar fashion to both of these other fields, but it developed into a different entity. The oldest portions, which are much re-worked and overlaid with later designs, are com-plicated groupings of simple linear figures, primary forms, whose special importance is only indicated by their concentration in a single location. On analysis, though, it can be seen that the figures relate overwhelmingly to birth, family and chil-dren, and that, as time went on, the people of Puakō began to use the lava field as a place to record the events of their lives—the news of the neighborhood.

One figure group is descriptive of an aliʻi, or chief's, birth. The carving of the father, robust and muscular, is almost three feet tall, attesting to his importance in the community. The mother, only slightly smaller, stands next to him with their daughter perched on her shoulder. Between them, suspended upside down from his father's hand and sheltered tenderly by his mother's arm, is the tiny newborn son who wears the crest of the ali'i. The carving is graphic; it is evocative, and it is curiously touching—like a family photograph of long-forgotten relatives. This is far more than a ritual design in the lava. These people seem to still live and breathe, and they are captured forever on a proud and happy day.

The best known petroglyph at Paniau shows a long line of marching men. Here twenty-nine figures in a single column snake their way toward the viewer. On either side of the line are large, important men, and nearby are several carvings that at first look like torsos. Professor J. Halley Cox, who did extensive research on the Puakō field in the 1950s, came to the conclusion that these were not meant to be people at all; rather, they represented the Lono, or harvest god, images normally carried in ceremonial processions. The position of the figure group near an ahupua'a boundary and the attendance of the ritual images marks the petroglyph probably not as a battle scene but rather as the representation of a makahiki procession. A periodic rite held to welcome tax collectors, this procession involved great ceremony and attendant celebrations in each ahupua'a. Games were held, feasts were given, kapus were relaxed, wars were suspended and then, at the height of the festivities,

Marchers, Puakō Petroglyph Field.

the tax collectors began their work. For the simple fishermen of Puakō, this must have been an occasion of mixed emotions, for the taxes themselves, which were owed to each layer of bureaucracy all the way up to the island aliʻis, were onerous; but the celebrations were the biggest, most exciting events of the season. And so the settlers painstakingly recorded the parade in the sooty black lava rock.

From time to time during the pre-European period, Puakō figured in the nightly news. In a culture with no written language, current events and items of philosophical speculation were recorded in legends and chants that passed orally from generation to generation, down the long, dark tunnels of time. Great battles were commemorated, great warriors were celebrated, the activities of the gods were noted, and, once in a while, there was a human-interest story. There seems to be a bit of each concerning Puakō.

The earliest scant mention of Puakō in legend concerns Madame Pele, the goddess of the volcano, who beached her canoe here on her arrival from Kauaʻi, declared it "a desolate spot", and journeyed on by foot to settle in the south. Later when the demi-god, Māui, concluded both his conquest of the island and his affair with Pele, his troops departed from Puakō on their way to Lānaʻi.

The canoe landing here was well known and figured again in the news during the invasion of the area by Kamalālāwalu from Maui. This invasion and the attendant battles between Kamalālāwalu and the local leaders, Lonoikamakahiki and Kanaloakuaana, on the plains below Waimea were landmark events in the history of the area. For a brief period, the saltmakers and fishermen were witness to grand warfare, and it did not go uncommemorated. Place names date from these battles, and comments on the warriors, the weather and the landscape entered into legend— and nothing as important happened again in Puakō until the time of Kamehameha the Great, nine generations later.

Kamalālāwalu had come from Maui with the hope of conquering the island of Hawai'i. He landed in advance of his troops at Kawaihae, and he asked advice on siting his major engagement. Two old local men, obviously without his best interests at heart, advised him to land his canoes on the broad beach at Puakō, "a place of eminence", and to destroy them so that his men could not retreat. They told him the best place to do battle with Lonoikamakahiki was on the plains northeast of the settlement. Kamalālāwalu was suspicious, and he worried about the clouds of red dust he saw swirling about. He read into it portents of blood and doom, but Kumaikeau, one of the local advisors, told him what every resident of Puakō has always known, that when the 'Ōlauniu wind of Puakō comes in contact with the wind from the north, a prodigious amount of dust is raised.

Against his better judgment, the chief planned his engagement, and soon a massive battle ebbed and flowed over the area. For a time the invaders appeared to have the upper hand. The brave local warrior, Kanaloakuaana, was captured, his tattooed eyes were gouged out, and he was slaughtered near the boat landing. From then on, the canoe beach has been called Kamakahiwa, or "totally black eye." Finally, however, the defenders prevailed, and Kamalālāwalu was slain "on the grassy plains of Puako [sic]." His soldiers, mistaking bait boxes moored offshore for canoes coming to their rescue, were trapped and butchered on our beach. This was our glorious moment and the closest Puakō ever came to participating directly in historical events.

In the social news, there is a legend that tells of, among other things, the saltmaking in Puakō. Five sisters from Kona were traveling north in search of husbands, and they paused near Kalāhuipua'a for the night. There the oldest of them, the beautiful Mailelauli'i, fell in love at first sight with a handsome saltmaker whose name was Puakō. Her feelings were reciprocated, and they married that same day. In the morning, the honeymoon over, Puakō was up early carrying heavy buckets of seawater to fill the shallow salt ponds which glistened in the hot morning sun. The bride's sisters, seeing him so occupied, were struck by the awful thought that if they lived here they would be conscripted to help at the salt works, and, if they had to work in the hot sun all day, they would eventually develop complexions that would look like the "windward bark of the noni tree." They were overcome with grief at the thought, and they wept and moaned and carried on until Mailelauli'i was forced to leave her handsome groom and travel on. Eventually they settled in Kohala, where she married the chief of the area of Pu'uepa and Hukia'a, and everyone, with the exception of poor Puakō, lived happily ever after.

And then we have the story of the Puakō town drunk and his thieving, unleashed dog, Pupualenalena. Master and dog had an arrangement whereby every night Pupualenalena stole 'awa from the Waipi'o Valley fields of Hakau, the king, and brought it home to the fisherman, who made a potent home-brew from the roots. In return, the fisherman fed the dog well from his daily catch. Eventually, the warriors of the king, investigating the thefts, saw Pupualenalena in the fields and tracked him home, where they identified his owner by his 'awa-scaly skin and drunken demeanor. The furious king first sentenced them both to death, but then relented on condition that Pupualenalena steal the conch-shell horn of the gods, who were keeping him awake at night with their intemperate trumpeting. The dog understood immediately, and that night he slipped into the house of the gods, thrust his head through the thong that held the conch and ran nimbly back to Hakau with the shell hanging around his neck. The king was so delighted that he granted the dog and his master a pardon and a plot of fertile land where they could raise their own 'awa and revel away together for the rest of their lives.

Except for the stuff of legends, we may assume that life was fairly quiet in Puakō. The population all along the coast grew over the years, reaching its high point around 1500. Our village at Puakō was but one of a number of shoreline settlements that stretched from Kawaihae to 'Anaeho'omalu. As time went on, the inland agricultural areas appear to have split off, and by 1650 there was formal and organized trade between the two areas.

It was no longer all in the family. To the north, Kawaihae was becoming rather industrialized as a center for canoe building. A Hawaiian court was frequently in residence there, and warriors trained for battle on the level plains nearby. Kalāhuipuaʻa and ʻAnaehoʻomalu, to the south, were both practicing aquaculture in their anchialine ponds, an industry so structured that some ponds were reserves for individual species of fish. But these were evolutionary changes in the neighborhood, not revolutionary, and life went on with remarkably little variation until the latter part of the eighteenth century. Then everything changed forever and our villagers at Puakō were visual witness to some of the most important events of the process.

Chapter III

CAPTAIN COOK,
KAMEHAMEHA
and the
FIRST EUROPEANS
1779 to 1835

Cook's final days
Pu'ukoholā: house for the gods
A great king's European advisors

In January of 1779, Captain James Cook, the famous British seaman and navigator, came ashore in Kealakekua on the Kona Coast of Hawai'i. He was the first European to sight and to land on the island of Hawai'i. After establishing relations with the Hawaiians under the chief Kalaniopu'u, charting the bay (which he called Karakakooa) and provisioning his ships, *Resolution* and *Discovery*, he sailed north with the intention of charting the Kohala Coast and then visiting the other islands. Shortly before the departure, he was visited on his flagship *Resolution* by a young nephew of the king, whose "elegant feathered cloake" was much admired by Cook's second officer, Clerke. This Hawaiian noble was Kamehameha, who had been advising his uncle during his negotiations with Cook and who, as Kamehameha the Great, was to unify all the islands of Hawai'i into a cohesive governmental body with himself as the

An artist's impression of a young Kamehameha, oil, by Robert Lyn Nelson.

ruling king. What each of these two men accomplished during his lifetime was to have profound implications for our little village.

Cook sailed past Puakō, close to shore, on February 6, and we can well imagine that everyone in the village was down on the beach on that windy day for their first look at Europeans. They were able to see the great, square-rigged ships standing off Kawaihae, where Cook sent William Bligh ashore

"Captain Cook", from a 19th-century engraving of the 1776 portrait by Nathaniel Dance.

in the *Resolution*'s small boat, together with a Hawaiian named Koa, to look for shelter and water. For some reason they found neither, but they did take some soundings of the harbor, which they understood to be named "Toeyahyah", and they rescued three village men whose canoe had overturned in rough water.

Bligh's party returned to the ships, which hove to offshore in steadily worsening weather. The *Resolution* remained in sight of Puakō, rolling and pitching through a series of violent squalls. Finally the two ships made sail north a short distance, but the mainmast of the *Resolution* snapped in the strong, gusty winds, and they were forced to limp back to Kealakekua for repairs. There the sailors found themselves unwelcome guests, having depleted the settlement's supplies during their recent reprovisioning. A series of misunderstandings and disputes led to an ugly confrontation on shore, during the course of which Cook was killed. Seventeen days after the first sighting, and much farther offshore, the ships, under the command of Clerke, passed Puakō again, tacked once near Māhukona and bore off mournfully toward Kahoʻolawe. It would be five years before the outside world read of the voyage and nine years before another European set foot on the island.

"Death of Captain Cook", from a 19th-century French engraving.

Here was history writ large (if delayed), and our little village was looking over the author's shoulder. Never a major participant, Puakō was still an active observer in events over the next sixty years that would turn upside down the social order, the practice of warfare, the foundations of learning, the base of economics and the religious tenets of the Hawaiian people. It is hard to imagine the scope of the adjustments that our small settlement of fishermen and saltmakers had to make so suddenly after six centuries of relative stability and order.

During the first years after the death of Cook, Kamehameha was becoming a force to be reckoned with in Hawai'i, and because he had been born in North Kohala and had ranged the Kohala Coast as a youth, Kawaihae was an important part of his power base. The plains behind the bay were his playing fields and a place where he could train his troops. The boatworks on Kawaihae beach produced many of the peleu, or war canoes, for his invasions, and the waters offshore were a favorite surfing spot.

At the same time, Kawaihae became a focus for the next European landings. When Cook's charts and journals were published in London in 1784, the only harbors that showed soundings were Kealakekua and Kawaihae. But substantial detail was shown for the portion of the shoreline from Kīholo north, and there were even references to coral shoals and indications of trees and the habitation at Puakō. This information led the next ships to call at the island, the American vessels the *Northwest America* and the *Iphigenia*, to anchor in Kawaihae harbor and to send men ashore. These ships, under Captains Russell and Douglas, respectively, were part of a fur-trading expedition that had gone ashore at Kaua'i in 1787 en route to Canton, returning by way of Alaska and the coast of British Columbia, where the *Northwest America* had been built. They carried with them, as a guest for the entire voyage from Kaua'i, a cousin of Kamehameha named Kaiana (or Taiana), and their arrival greeting at Kawaihae in October of 1788 was tumultuous. The events were described by John Meares, an officer aboard another ship to arrive at that time, the *Nootka*.

"The great mountain, or Mouna Kaah [Mauna Kea], . . . was clothed in clouds . . . from its base to the sea was a beautiful amphitheatre [sic] of villages and plantations, while the shore was crowded with people, who, from the coolness of the morning, were clothed in their party-coloured [sic] garments. Some of them were seated on the banks to look at the ship, while others were running along the shore toward the little sandy patches where the canoes were drawn up, in order to come off to us. We now hove to in the entrance of Teo-yah-yah Bay. Nor was it long before a considerable number of canoes came off . . . [bearing] hogs, pigs, taro—etc. . . . Before night, upwards of 400 hogs were purchased, decks were loaded, and the boats filled with them and the vegetables. Among the multitude which visited us . . . was . . . one person of rank. He came in a double canoe paddled along by 12 men . . . [and had with him] his wife and 2 young female children. He brot [sic] very large hogs and a large quantity of cocoa-nuts [sic], and immediately followed his present, accompanying it with the most friendly expressions and offers of further service." The service went both ways, for during the happy visit of the ships, Kamehameha traded with Captain Russell for some muskets, a cannon, ammunition and instruction in their use. They were to provide him both a technical and psychological edge over his future opponents.

At the time of the visit of the American ships, Kamehameha had only one enemy left on the island of Hawai'i, his cousin Keōua. He was advised to attack Keōua indirectly, by building a house for the gods, and so the construction of the great heiau, Pu'ukoholā, was undertaken just south of Kawaihae. The labor was conscripted from every rank of Hawaiian and from every village and hamlet in the area. Even Kamehameha himself performed manual labor carrying stones. A camp was set up on the mauka plains between today's Spencer Park and Mauna Kea Resort for several thousand workers. From the little Puakō settlement near the present main road, it would have been possible to view the vast encampment which covered the level ground and the rising hillsides toward Mauna Kea, as well as the lines of workers, stretching into the distance, passing stones in a continuous chain from hand to hand to the masons at the construction site.

Puakō provided workers for the project and also

food, mainly coconuts. This cannot have been easy
for a community that demanded hard work from
its inhabitants just to feed itself. To lose a large
portion of the workforce together with a great part
of the food supply must have been a great hard-
ship, but the commands of the aliʻi were immuta-
ble laws. The supply of coconuts proved to be
delicious, and later, when Kamehameha was in
Waimea reconstructing the Uli heiau, Puakō was
called upon to provide all the coconuts for the dedi-
cation. When it appeared there would not be
enough, Kamehameha and one of his followers
went back to Puakō under cover of darkness (so
that the chief would not be seen working) and
carried four hundred and eighty nuts in two enormous nets up the mountain to Waimea.

The construction of Puʻukoholā took more than
a year, and during the period of construction,
Kamehameha's enemies tried to defeat his cause
in a great naval battle off the northeast coast of
the island. Kamehameha's forces prevailed, and,
ultimately, Keōua surrendered. Kamehameha,
through intermediaries, invited him to the dedi-
cation of the heiau, and, although his advisors
counseled him not to go, Keōua accepted both the
invitation and its implications and set forth by
water up the west coast of the island.

The evening before he was to arrive at Kawaihae, his party camped on the beach south of Puakō, and he performed certain rituals which made it clear to his followers that he expected to die. All Puakō watched Keōua pass the next day on his great double canoe, escorted by twenty-seven smaller boats, in shallow water just offshore. He was regally dressed and surrounded by his nobles, one of whom bore the kāhili, the torch-like symbol of Keōua's rank. Ahead were the massed war canoes of Kamehameha, which were arrayed in a vast half circle below the walls of Puʻukoholā, and Keōua's flotilla paddled slowly and with great dignity toward the scene of its destruction. Upon arrival in front of the heiau, the warriors of Kamehameha fell upon the boats, and not a single warrior was spared. Keōua was interred in great secrecy in Puakō at Paniau. So well was the stone placed at the entrance to his burial cave that no one has ever discovered the tomb. His death marked the end of any resistance to Kamehameha, and the passing of power on the island to the most influential Hawaiian in history.

Shortly before this, Hawaiʻi had acquired its first European residents, Isaac Davis and John Young. The two men were British and Welsh respectively but serving aboard American ships, the

Eleanora and the *Fair American*. The ships were owned (and the *Eleanora* skippered) by Captain Simon Metcalfe, an extraordinarily rough and cruel man with a history of bloody confrontations with the Hawaiian natives. In Olowalu Bay, he turned the ship's cannons on local villagers who had come to trade with the *Eleanora*, and, in retaliation, the chief of Kealakekua vowed revenge on the next foreign ship to enter the bay.

So it was that when the *Fair American*, skippered by Metcalfe's son and counting Davis among the crew, anchored in that bay, it was boarded by the chief and his men, and a slaughter ensued. Davis was the sole survivor of the attack. Badly wounded, the sailor nevertheless was able to get to land, where Kamehameha took him prisoner, and his life was spared. At this same time, Young was ashore from the *Eleanora*. Because of the altercation, there was no communication between the village and the ship, and the *Eleanora* sailed off without him. Davis and Young were initially regarded as prisoners of Kamehameha, but as time went on, they earned the trust of the king and Kamehameha took both men into his service. Davis eventually moved to Oʻahu, where the king had granted him land.

John Young stayed on the Island of Hawaiʻi and

became a profound influence on the relationship of the Hawaiian monarchy with the outside world. He was essentially a good and decent man, and he became a trusted advisor to, and agent for, the king, an association that endured until the death of Kamehameha in 1819. He was popular with the Hawaiians, who nicknamed him "Olohana", because when he had been boatswain of the *Eleanora* they had heard him calling the order "All hands." He married twice, the second time to a niece of Kamehameha, his first wife having died of cholera in 1804.

Young chose to settle in Kawaihae and built the first house there in the European style in 1798. It was constructed of coral blocks cut from the reef at Puakō and brought by canoe to the site. The roof was thatched, and the house was described as being airy and comfortable on its pleasant, cool site which overlooked the anchorage. Ruins of the foundation can still be seen below Puʻukoholā. The explorer Kotzebue described the property a few years later: "Near Tocahai [Kawaihae] Bay, when the wind entirely died down . . . we saw Young's settlement of several houses built of white stone, after the European fashion, surrounded by palm and banana trees."

When George Vancouver hauled into Kawaihae

Bay in 1792, John Young greeted him, along with
Kamehameha. Vancouver noted anchoring on a
"brown sand bottom with some small pieces of
coral. The adjacent shores seemed to be very fruit-
ful, whilst a number of inhabitants indicated them
to be well peopled."

The presence of John Young at Kawaihae encouraged foreign visits and commerce to this part of the
coast. From the simple offerings of hogs and fruit
in return for nails and iron objects, trade became
more organized. John Young, as the king's repre-
sentative, acted as a purchasing agent, procuring
supplies and setting prices. The Russian ship *Neva*
noted in 1804 that coins were now in use and that
the Hawaiians were even charging in silver to put
travelers up for the night. "The island of Owhee [sic]
has undergone, within the last ten yrs., a very considerable change. Everything at present is dear, on
account of many American ships, which, in navigat-
ing these waters, always touch at the Sandwich
Islands for refreshments. In the course of a
twelvemonth, the Bay of Caracacooa [sic] has been
visited by no less than eighteen different vessels."

Puakō benefited from this new trade; salt was
made here, and there was an increasing demand
for the product. The community already had the
habit of trade, for, unlike many of the ahupa'as,

they were not self-sufficient, and they had always bartered their salt, their seafood and their fine lauhala mats for vegetables and other necessities. Now this trade went beyond the neighbors. Some of the salt was bought by the ships to trade with the Russians on the northwest coast of America. More often the salt was used by the ships to cure pork and fish. As time went on, the Hawaiians began to prepare the provisions themselves. Captain Jennings, around 1814, mentions people employed on shore near Puakō "killing and salting pork," and that he traded for island rope "which makes excellent running rigging."

Because of the configuration of the reef at that time, ships putting into the harbor tacked in close to shore south of Hāpuna Bay and followed a fathom line (a course on a nautical chart connecting areas of equal depth) from there to an anchorage immediately north of Puʻukoholā, not too far from the site of the present barge harbor and almost a mile offshore. So it was that the average resident of Puakō, lugging water to his salt ponds, was frequently treated to the spectacular sight of a square-rigged ship scudding in toward shore, dropping much of her sail and inching up the coast toward Kawaihae.

At this same time, an important trade in sandalwood developed. While it did not affect Puakō directly, it attracted more ships to Kawaihae, where much of the timber was loaded, and increased their trade in provisions. There was a vast forest of sandalwood on the slopes of Mauna Kea, the extent of which is hard to visualize today. Kotzebue described the landscape from the sea. "The declivities appear bare & sun-burnt. Some parts are used for tillage, the most are covered with scanty grass. Amidst the clouds, the region of the forest begins, & the eye scarcely reaches the naked crowns of the gigantic Mountain."

Two to three thousand workers were employed carrying sandalwood to the beach at Kawaihae for loading to be shipped to Oʻahu. John Young served as pilot for the incoming ships, weighmaster and accountant. The price was given in Spanish dollars, and, in 1815 was equal to $8.50 in United States dollars per picquel, a measure of close to 150 pounds. The neighborhood was thriving, in the western, commercial sense of the word, and the population of Puakō shared in the bounty. The number of villagers was seen to increase during this time. By 1835, its population was greater than that of Kawaihae. This era was the economic high point in the history of our community.

Chapter IV

THE
MISSIONARIES
APPEAR
1823 to 1895

Lorenzo Lyons, beloved of Hawaiians
Disease and a shrinking population
Evening Star church: Hōkūloa

On August 23, 1823, Puakō received a visit that opened the next chapter in its westernization. Around sunset, Asa Thurston, a Christian missionary, came down the trail from Waikoloa and asked for shelter for the night.

He was one of a group of four Christian missionaries who had been circling the island since June on a survey to ascertain the advisability of establishing stations there. The other members of the party, William Ellis, Artemus Bishop and Joseph Goodrich, had gone on to Kailua, leaving Thurston to conduct an independent exploration and enumeration of the settlements around Kawaihae and Waimea. Thurston already had spent a night at John Young's house before he set out for the mountainside habitations, and word traveled quickly among the villages, so he did not arrive completely unannounced. Nor was it unusual for European travelers to be received for the night, but on the following morning, an unprecedented event occurred in Puakō. Thurston assembled the residents of our community, which he described as "a considerable village", and brought them the word of Christ. It is difficult to imagine what their reaction must have been. Recent events would have encouraged acceptance of the sermon. Hawaiian religious beliefs and practices had been somewhat undermined by the abolition of various kapus shortly after the death of Kamehameha in 1819. Missionaries had preached in Kailua-Kona in 1820–1821 and were a continuing presence on Oʻahu. Also, John Young, an accepted and respected neighbor, was a friendly supporter of the ministers.

Even so, there is no evidence to suggest that the people of Puakō were in any way prepared for conversion. Nor is there any evidence to suggest that Asa Thurston, who was a staunch supporter of alcoholic abstinence and strict monogamy, was in any way prepared for our village, which was no more devoted to these virtues than the others of the island. All we know today, from the church records, is that when Lorenzo Lyons, the pre-eminent missionary for the area, came to Waimea in the early 1830s to join the local station, there was both an active congregation and a school in Puakō and that these fell under his ministry.

Lorenzo Lyons and his wife Betsy were, respectively, twenty-four and eighteen years old when they arrived in Kawaihae on the *Arrick* in 1832. One month later, Lorenzo preached his first sermon in the Hawaiian language in Waimea. They were to devote the rest of their lives to the people of the northern portion of the island of Hawai'i. For Betsy, this was to be only six years; she died in 1838, probably from complications after influenza.

For Lorenzo, the beloved "Makua Laiana" of the Hawaiians, it was an association that was to last until his death in 1886. From the base of his ministry in Waimea, Lyons traveled on foot, by canoe, by horse, even (in his later years) across deep streams on the strong backs of his Hawaiian companions. He journeyed between Honoka'a and the Waipi'o Valley on the east coast to Kawaihae and Puakō on the west coast spreading the gospel, ministering to the sick and needy and establishing schools and churches, at first in native hales, later in structures of increasing solidarity, size and permanence. His records to the American Board of Ecumenical Missions, the annual *Waimea Report*, preserved today in the Hawaiian Mission Children's Society Library, provide concerned and affectionate descriptions of our little community.

Lorenzo Lyons. Credit: Hawaiian Mission Children's Society Library, Mission Houses Museum.

The first of these reports was written in the fall
of 1835, after he had spent several days in
Kawaihae holding meetings. He decided to walk to
Puakō early in the morning, "along the shore—
alone. On one hand was the ocean; on the other a
dreary, desolate waste—rocks, lava, coral. . . . I
reached Puako [sic] at an early hour. As I was alone
and carrying my own calabash, the natives mis-
took me for some wandering foreigner, and when
I spoke to them in their own language, how star-
tled they were! But some knew me. They expressed
a great deal of pity for me because I had to carry
my own baggage. It was amusing to hear their
conversation about it. A missionary, they think,
should be exactly like their chiefs.

"A strange thing indeed it would be that the
traveling missionary should be accompanied by a
train of attendants, as the chiefs are!

"I excited a great deal of curiosity, I then had
breakfast—that is, sat on a stone [probably across
the street from where the condominium building
stands today] and ate a biscuit. No water could be
had but salt water. As soon as the people could be
collected together I talked to them; examined their
school, after which took a look at the salt works,
took dinner, drank some coconut water, and started
for home, my horse having come after me. [Horses

frequently were left to follow after the rider, who walked on foot over the lava paths in the early morning, or evening hours, when it was dark and much cooler.]

"Puako [sic] is a village on the shore, very like Kawaihae, but larger. It has a small harbor in which native vessels anchor. Coconut groves give it a verdant aspect. No food grows in the place. The people make salt and catch fish. These they exchange for vegetables grown elsewhere."

In December of 1841 he writes that he spent two days in Puakō and "visited every house in the place—held several meetings excommunicated 66 [!]—suspended 3—restored 3—held a communion season—45 communicants—ascertained deaths, births, removals during the year—& the present population." In 1844 he notes that he "found a very encouraging state of things. . . . Many hardened backsliders had been brot [sic] to repentance—& many of the wicked both old & young had professedly forsaken their wicked ways & turned to the Lord." He remarks that at Kawaihae the women wore "bonnets & English dresses" and that the meetinghouse was "well furnished with mats & seats." In 1853 he preached at Puakō, in heavy rain under a leaking roof, while holding an umbrella over his head.

During the years of his reports, Lyons documents a steady decline in the fortunes of the inhabitants of Puakō. In part it was due to the normal hazards of fishing for a living, but a great deal of the blame was to be found in the system of taxation. Everything and everyone was taxed: unborn children, olana (hemp), sandalwood, salt, fish, salted fish, hogs, dogs and feathers, to name but a few of the items. Vast numbers of work days, for which there was no recompense, were levied by the king, the chiefs and the headmen of the ahupua'as (konohikis). Moreover, Puakō was now dependent on the Kohala area for provisions, which were brought down the coast by boat, and they were charged exorbitant prices for produce. Lyons wrote in 1844 that during his church inspection tour, "Thanksgiving feasts were observed . . . & . . . [one] was appointed in Puako [sic]—but the poor people of that place could not raise fish & poi enough for such a purpose. . . . I never ate nor drank anything while there." The residents could no longer afford oil to light their hales at night, and he held at least one prayer meeting "by the light of Venus, aided eventually by that of the moon."

There was a steady decline in the population of the whole area. In 1820 the South Kohala–Hāmākua population was estimated at ten thousand. By

1863 it had shrunk to three thousand. In addition
to population movement due to lessening economic
gains, western diseases had taken a toll. The whaling fleet called regularly at Kawaihae during the
1850s, and the greater exposure to outside commerce brought with it greater exposure to illness.
Several epidemics of influenza, measles and
whooping cough were documented. In 1853 there
was a major smallpox epidemic. It swept the area,
spreading from Waimea to Kawaihae and Puakō.
Vaccine was made available through a public-
health committee sponsored by the mission, and
Lyons tirelessly inoculated the population of
Waimea. Humphreys, the chairman of the local
committee, came by boat to Puakō to offer protection to the residents, but he was not permitted to
land. To a man, the residents refused the shots, and
they survived the epidemic by sealing themselves
off from the rest of the world. No canoes came
ashore at the landing; no one was allowed access
by trail, and only after the pestilence subsided was
anyone welcome in the settlement, and, even then,
only after a lengthy quarantine imposed by the
elders of the village.

The strategy worked, and Puakō was spared the
worst of the epidemic, but our community gained
a reputation for clannishness and unfriendly

behavior that long outlasted the immediate danger. Perhaps it was worth it. After Lyons visited Kawaihae in the wake of the scourge, all he could say was, "Where [are] the aged? Where [are] the young?" The population there had been decimated.

King Kamehameha III gave a piece of his own royal lands in Puakō to Lorenzo Lyons for the use of his ministry, and in 1858 work commenced on our church, which was to be named Hōkūloa, or evening star. The men of the parish volunteered the labor. A twenty-one by thirty-six foot foundation was laid, and divers cut and brought up coral blocks from the Puakō reef, which were fired in pits, ground and mixed with sand and water to make mortar to bind the rock walls. Floor planks were cut and hewed from koa and hauled down from the high forests. Lorenzo Lyons' report of 1859 provides some detail:

"I reported this [church] last year as on the way—the stone walls up—laid in mortar—& windows procured. This is the poorest parish in my field, rendered still poorer of late by the frequent rains that have prevented the people from making salt—one of their chief dependencies—the wind—rough weather, & the heat of the volcanic stream that entered the sea near this place [from the enormous 1859 eruption of Mauna Loa, from which lava flowed over twenty-five miles to this coast] have killed or frightened away all their fish the 2nd source of wealth. There remain the fruit of a few cocoa nut [sic] trees, & the lauhala from the leaf of which the women busy themselves in making mats. The men can sometimes find a job of work that will bring them in something, i.e. if they can manage to obtain food, all of which comes from a distance. One such job they have found. They have built a stone schoolhouse plastered inside and out & surrounded it with a stone wall, & turned all the avails 120$ [sic] into their [church] [This school building stood on the shoreline immediately north of the church]. The avails of the women's mats are disposed of in the same way. With the funds obtained & any others I may be so fortunate as to secure by begging or otherwise, I am authorized by the trustees to purchase materials for the roof - floor &c. We have resolved to have the roof & belfrey & the floor laid by the next communion season—which is the last week in Aug."

There is a watercolor from 1859 by Paul Emmert, a Swiss artist and resident of Kailua-Kona, that shows three vast fountains of the Mauna Loa eruption on the horizon, with some of the houses, the school building and the half-completed church, surrounded by scaffolding, on the shoreline. It must have been a horrible year for our little village, and it was an amazing display of spirit in the midst of adversity that kept the construction going in this time of depredation.

On March 21, 1860, Hōkūloa church was dedicated, and a fine new bell in its little steeple replaced the conch shell horn that had formerly called the faithful to worship. Lyons describes the scene with satisfaction. "The stone chh [sic], with its whitened walls, & reddened roof & humble spire give the place an air of civilization & religiousness, & the school house in close proximity with its similar walls tho' thatched roof, makes something of a show." The seventy-member parish held a festival to help pay off the remaining $1,200 debt.

For the next years, the annual reports note only passing news of the community as it continued its gradual decline. Barenaba K, the sub pastor, was found to be not highly qualified for the job. The schoolteacher, a "smart young man", fell and was injured. He was replaced by an older fellow "whom the last examination shows to be incompetent for his position." A mother and daughter were burned to death in a house fire, and that same year a deacon of the church, a carpenter, died. He had been at the center of a scandal that must have had all the parish tongues clacking. His "perfidious

"Puakō, Kohala, Hawai'i", watercolor, by Paul Emmert, 1859. Photograph

Honolulu Academy of Arts, Gift of Mary Alexander Smith, 1990.

wife . . . basely deserted him" for a "feindish [sic] paramour" [according to Lyons] who somehow negotiated a divorce, married her and "lived with her for years, in the very presence as it were, of the innocent & vitally injured husband." Lyons fairly sputters as he recounts how, even after he had excommunicated the guilty lovers, "no shadow of penitence has darkened or saddened their brow[s] from the committal of the act to the present."

That same year, a "declension in the attendance on meetings" was noted, and, although the church had been well kept, the parish had given up some of the regular services. Somehow it seemed as if, gradually, the spirit had gone out of our little village. In 1884, under the guidance of the Reverend Jonathon Stupplebeen, the church underwent a considerable restoration and it was rededicated January 1, 1885. But still its fortunes declined.

Although Kawaihae Uka, the inland portion of that settlement, was thriving—in part by raising Irish potatoes and selling them to the whaling ships for $7,000 a year—it was not thought possible to turn the sandy, salty soil of Puakō to agricultural use. At least not until a great discovery in 1895 when a bit of sugar cane was found growing wild.

Chapter V

RAISING CANE— THE SUGAR PLANTATION 1895 to 1914

'Fine, up-to-date little mill'
A jaunty, brass-trimmed engine
Crushing defeat

Sugar cane had been grown on the Kohala side of the Big Island since about 1825, and two Chinese immigrants were growing and processing cane in 1827 in the area that today is dryside Waimea. Although Hawaiians had grown sugar cane in modest quantities for centuries, it was mainly the European and American settlers on Oʻahu, Maui and the Big Island who seized on the idea of cultivating it commercially. The first major operation on this side of the island, the Kohala Sugar Company, was incorporated in 1863 in Halaʻula, North Kohala. Robert Hind developed the Hāwī Mill & Plantation Co., Ltd. around 1880, and was soon doing well enough to be interested in expanding to other areas.

Hind's son, John, described in his journals the chance discovery of wild sugar cane that led to the establishment of a sugar-cane plantation in Puakō in 1895.

"Mr. W. I. Vredenberg one Sunday came to Hawi in a state of considerable excitement, with four or five sticks of fine looking cane strapped to his saddle, which, as he put it, he discovered at Puakō the day before while on a shooting trip. This cane was grown without irrigation, and he enthusiastically announced there were large areas of as good land as that on which these sticks were grown.... Conditions appeared extremely favorable.... Soil was analyzed ... a well was sunk (about ten feet) water analyzed and found to contain no more salt water than other plantations, using well water. An experimental plot was planted, which for growth exceeded anything I had ever seen."

At this juncture, the Hind family entered into negotiations with the Parker Ranch. The Parker family had bought some of the Lunalilo royal lands in Puakō for use as a winter range for cattle and to facilitate the occasional shipping of their animals from Puakō Bay. Robert and John Hind were able to trade a piece of property they held in the

Hilo area for a swath of land in Puakō, all but one-sixteenth of the Parker Ranch holdings. They held this land until the 1950s, when the family sold it back to the Parker Ranch. Additional acreage was leased from the territory. The plantation eventually included the site of the present boat ramp, a piece of the shoreline, and between 1500 and 1800 acres of the present kiawe forests east of today's Puakō Beach Drive.

Norman G. Campion, a marine engineer, was hired to design and construct a mill. Access by land being difficult, a wharf was built first, just south of the present-day boat ramp. It was to be used by lighters ferrying processed sugar to freighters waiting offshore and as the dock for the gasoline-powered "Puako steamer", an ocean-going tug with a captain noted for his weakness for alcoholic beverages. Then, as John Hind wrote, "A fine up to date little mill with all the appurtenances which go with a modern plantation was installed, on an ideal site, a hundred or so yards from the landing." It held the crushing machinery, the mixers, the vats and the rest of the mechanical necessities. In addition to the plant, dormitories and a camp for over three hundred workers, a company store, two schoolhouses (the second a small building used as a Japanese school), an office building, various storage

Puakō Sugar Mill, with snow capped Mauna Kea in background.

and warehouse facilities and a shed for honey-processing machinery were built. This last was to support a beekeeping operation on the plantation land.

Along with the mill construction, a two-foot gauge rail line was laid, mostly along the shore, extending about a mile from the wharf to a terminus just north of Waimā Point. A jaunty little 0-4-0T engine, all shiny black paint and gleaming brass trim, was commissioned from the H. K. Porter Company and

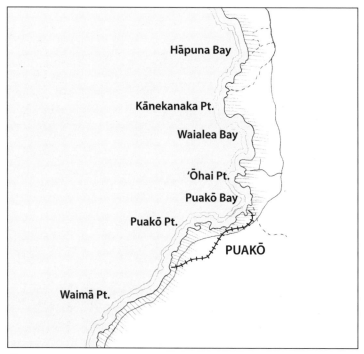

Sugar train route. The track bed appears to have covered a distance of about one mile.

delivery was taken in March 1902. It was named the "Puako", and soon it was chugging up and down the shore carrying cane to the mill and supplies to the fields. The railbed can still be seen in places. Because the shoreline has subsided, the

Remnants of track bed at low tide north of Waimā Point.

sites are now in shallow water on the lava just north of Waimā Point.

The same Wilmot Vredenberg who had found the first sugar cane was hired to manage the plantation for the Hind family. He may have been Puakō's first resident haole, and his life would make a book in itself. He was British, but had arrived on the island as supercargo on a steamer, shepherding a group of Portuguese immigrants from France. He had been so miserably seasick during the passage that he vowed never to leave land again. As a joke, the Hawaiians nicknamed him "Manuwai", or seabird, and he was to be called this for the rest of his life. He found various occupations on the island: at one point he taught school and he also started a ranch in Waimea, where he raised strawberries. Manuwai is said to have had a genial disposition, a great many friends and an unusual ability to play the cornet with one hand while accompanying himself on the piano with the other. He was the nearest thing to an orchestra that the Kohala area could muster; he often played for dances there, arriving on horseback, tootling on his cornet as he rode down the trail. When he took over the mill, he built a house for himself and his wife in Puakō. It has been described by John Hind as a "home near the sea a feature of which was a floored outdoor space thirty or forty feet square, open on three sides the fourth being the house proper, and roofed with coconut fronds. Such an overlarge porch is known in Hawaii [sic] as a 'lanai.'"

Another visitor to Puakō, Jack Hall, who did clerical work for the plantation from time to time, wrote, "Right close to the plantation was a beautiful stretch of sand. . . . On the point was a large grove of coconut palms, in which were three grass houses, occupied by Hawaiians. Manuwai's house was right on the beach overlooking the bay with a very large lanai walled and roofed with native matting, and the view at sundown, when the great golden orb sank slowly into the ocean, was simply gorgeous."

Hall goes on to describe a visit from Puakō's first, but certainly not last, beachcomber: "Manuwai and I were sitting on the lanai one afternoon when a man came along the beach from the direction of Kona and, stopping, addressed my friend in fluent Hawaiian. He seemed under the influence of liquor, was barefooted, wearing only a shabby pair of trousers, a shirt and a hat, and from the color of his skin and proficiency in Hawaiian, I thought he was a half-white. After the man departed, Manuwai gave me a little of his history. His name was Smith, he was of good Scottish family, well educated and, at one time, had been employed by the Bank of Scotland. He had held good positions in Honolulu but lost them and now lived along the beach from Kawaihae to the end of Kona, sleeping and eating anywhere he could with the natives. . . . It seemed such a pity for a man like that to have lost his grip and become a beachcomber."

The mill, when it opened, employed a large resident workforce of Hawaiians, Japanese, Chinese and Filipinos, and for a time it looked as if the fortunes of our little community were finally on the way up again. However, almost from the very beginning, the plantation had problems.

The first planting, probably in 1901, was all but wiped out by a flood that was caused when some of the intermittently running streams overflowed their banks. While later the alluvial soil was to prove an asset, it was a disaster for the newly planted fields. Then the problem was compounded by those famous Puakō winds. Hind reported, "During the first year or two we only had a couple of severe visitations [of wind], but later, while we

"Puako" Steam locomotive, Hawai'i, circa 1935. Photograph. Bishop Museum.

Derelict remains of Puakō Plantation locomotive "Puako" at Dillingham Quarry, Waipahu, Oʻahu, circa 1946.

might be exempt for several months and everything flourishing, we would have a continuation of storms which, at times, would threaten to blow us off the map. . . . I have seen the property more than once look good for . . . amounts . . . of $35,000 $50,000 a year; after a three day blow look like 'thirty cents'."

The drying effect of the wind left salt behind in the soil that could not be leached out by subsequent irrigation, and there was not enough rainfall on the dry coast to do the job naturally. Finally, after a thorough investigation of the water flow of the Waimea stream, an eight-mile flume was constructed to carry fresh water for the fields to Puakō. Ironically, the stream failed just before the flume was completed. Generations of logging sandalwood in the mountains had destroyed the watershed and altered the climate. This was the death knell for the plantation and marked the low ebb of fortune for our community.

In 1913 the mill machinery and tanks were removed and some of them were installed at the Hind mill in Hōʻea. Part of the equipment was lost during shipment when the vessel *Kauaʻi* went down on Christmas Eve, 1913, in the harbor at Māhukona. The crushing equipment was later sold to the Ormoc Sugar Company on Leyte in the Philippines, where it was still operating fifty years after its manufacture. Puakō, the little engine, was sold to the Dillingham Quarry on Oʻahu, where it was used to haul rock for a number of years. It was eventually abandoned in the lower Pouhala Canyon after it was stranded there when a bridge collapsed. It was photographed by Malcolm Gaddis and Kent

Cochrane in 1946, derelict and covered with vines. In 1982 the same train buffs found and photographed her again by hiking two miles through the brush, and they reported that there was no longer enough of her left to salvage. And so, in disarray and rust, the last vestige of the sugar plantation disappeared.

Derelict remains of locomotive "Puako." 1982.

Chapter VI

STARTING
OVER
1914 to 1969

Ring in a shark's stomach
Lost barrel of home-brew
The bee business

When the sugar mill closed, only about seven families remained behind in Puakō. Any larger sense of community was gone. The church no longer held services and fell into disrepair, eventually losing its roof. The schoolhouse burned, and nothing was done to rebuild it; the few children remaining went to Kawaihae, Waimea or Kona for their education. There is no record of what happened to Vredenberg's comfortable home on the bay, but the mill buildings, with the exception of two warehouses, were either taken down or fell down, leaving only cement foundations and floors. Even the little cemetery that had been established up on the hill was abandoned, the last burial there occurring in 1917. But if the old settlement

Hōkūloa Church, Puakō, 1906. Credit: Hawaiian Mission Children's Society Library, Mission Houses Museum.

disappeared, those who stayed on became the bridges to the residential community we know today.

Of the remaining people, the Pai and Purdy family, great-grandparents of Henry Auwae, the noted practitioner and teacher of traditional Hawaiian medicine, continued to live up on the hill near what is now the highway. The other households established themselves near the water, ranging along the bay from the old mill property to just south of the church.

Nearest to the remains of the milling operation was the residence of the Goto family. Asakichi Goto, the father, had come from Japan in the late

1800s as a contract laborer earning 12½ cents a day in the fields of the Hāmākua Coast. He had gone back to Japan to marry and had returned to Kona, together with his wife and their first-born son. At about that time the Puakō plantation was hiring workers, and he signed on. At first they lived in the workers' camp, but when Hind's beekeeper died, Asakichi was asked to take over the honey operation. The family, which eventually consisted of five children, moved to a primitive house on the piece of mill property where the bee house was located. When the mill closed, they continued to make honey under contract to Robert Hind. They eventually bought the property in 1924 for $35,000, along with the beehives, honey houses and extractors, several cows, one bull, a few market-able hogs and a sizeable boat. Family members continued to occupy that site until the 1960s, and another property on Puakō Beach Drive until the late 1990s. Ichiro Goto, the middle son, kept a journal for many years, and his writings provide ongoing and engaging descriptions of daily life in Puakō.

The original Goto house was a twenty-four by fourteen foot rectangle with newspapers for wall-paper and a tin roof. The only furniture was one chair at a sewing machine, and there was a barrel of home-brew in the corner. One portion of the floor

Asakichi and Nami Goto, 1930s (originally came to Puakō in 1902).

was elevated about eighteen inches and was covered with sleeping mats; it was here that the family gathered. A second two-room shack fifty feet away held the kitchen and dining room. There was no running water in either house, but there was a shallow well nearby that filled with brackish water at high tide. The cooking was done over an open fire in pots hanging from an iron rod resting on flat stones.

The next house to the south belonged to the Kaono family, a sprawling Hawaiian clan that was originally from Maui. The grandparents continued in Puakō until 1934 in a house with a deep lanai where the grandchildren slept during family summers. The children ran naked on the beach in the hot, white sunlight and swam in the warm water all day, happy occupants of a private Eden.

Next door to the Kaono property was a piece of land that belonged to Jack Paulo (sometimes called "Paulo Nuhi"), whose wife, Annie, was a member of the Laau family. He appeared to have lived in various other sites ranging from Kawaihae to Kalāhuipua'a, always in grass houses. He was the last person in the area to live in the traditional Hawaiian way, and he became the final guardian of local Hawaiian lore. When the Kaono grandmother and grandfather died, in 1933 and 1934, it was Jack Paulo who presided at their interments in the ancient burial caves in Puakō, the last ever to take place there. He was the only person who knew the chants that accompanied the moving of the stones that sealed the caves.

Evidently Paulo toyed with the idea of sharing at least some of this knowledge with Ichiro Goto, who described the event as follows: "When old man David Kaono died we all took him to Nuhi's burial cave in Puakō. And as we gathered around the opening of the cave's entrance, Paulo picked [me]

Ichiro and Yukie Goto, family and friends, in donkey cart, 1940s.

from the people who attended the event [to follow him into the cave]. His explanation at that time was for someone he could trust . . . whom they all can trust. At that burial [site] there were two caves. One was already full with the original occupaints [sic] and . . . sealed. [In] the other one . . . just over the doorway there is a skeleton wrapped in tapa cloth . . . a maiden . . . guarding the people buried there. [The cave] is filled with many valuables, such as gold and silver and jewels." However, Paulo never shared the chants and rituals with Goto, and ironically, when Jack Paulo died in the 1940s he was buried in the Veterans' Cemetery, for there was no one left who knew the secrets of the caves.

Just south of the Hōkūloa Church was a piece of kuleana land. Kuleanas were lands that were claimed by resident Hawaiians at the time of the Great Mahele in 1848, a system set in place to provide title to Hawaiian property in a western style of ownership. Before this time, all land was held in trust by the aliʻi, who controlled its use through their konohiki, usually lesser chiefs who functioned as land agents for the kings. Under the Mahele, the land was divided between the crown, the government, the konohiki and certain native tenants, who could file claims for lands they lived on and worked "for the welfare of the earth." Rough boundaries were set up for the kuleanas dependent on landmarks (walls, trees, rocks, etc.), which were later refined by surveys. The claim for the property south of the church stated, "Akahi claimed one house lot on the shore enclosed by a stone wall from ancient times." Two other claims in Puakō were recorded, one next to the Paulo property and another on the shoreline behind the church.

The Akahi kuleana was owned by the Akona family, who occupied an impressively large stone house there. A house of this size and construction was most unusual for anyone not of royalty or great wealth, and there is a local legend which explains it. Actually, several local legends explain it, as diverse in detail as local memories, but the basic story seems to be that two members of the Akona family caught a shark off Puakō. When they opened it, they found a ring in its stomach, and they advertised in the newspaper for its owner. A man whose daughter had disappeared in Hawaiian waters answered the ad, and he was so grateful for the return of her ring that he rewarded the fishermen handsomely. The family decided to use the money to build a fine house as a tribute to the woman and to their sudden good fortune. This house stood until 1980, when new owners demolished it to clear space for the Whale's Tail, a condominium project.

Ruins of Akona coral house.

With the closure of the sugar mill, regular boat service to Puakō stopped, and the residents were left in semi-isolation. The only access by land was the historic trail from Kawaihae, which had been widened to accommodate horses and stock drives, but was nevertheless a long, unpleasant trek. The upper road from Waimea met the trail at what is now Spencer Beach State Park, and from there the trail to our settlement required the traveler to ford several streams, traverse Kauna'oa and Hāpuna beaches and then cut inland behind Waialea Bay, arriving at Puakō in the general vicinity of the present-day dump. No improvements were made until 1931, when a two-week clearing project cleaned up the trail from Kawaihae to Kalāhuipuaʻa. Even then, the trip to Kawaihae and the nearest store, on horseback, took a minimum of three hours. A trip to Kona was a journey of several days, with overnight stops at ʻAnaehoʻomalu, Kīholo, Kaʻūpūlehu and Keāhole. Puakō was a favorite overnight stopping place for the few travelers coming from farther north, in part because there was a group of brigands at Kalāhuipuaʻa in the early part of the century who were thought to have robbed and murdered more than one camper there, and rumor had it that more people than Hawaiians occupied its burial caves. It was an area best traversed in daylight hours.

The major portion of what little traffic there was to and from Puakō moved by water. There was still a wharf left from the sugar mill, and it was far easier to bring in supplies by boat than by trail. The vessels of choice were sampans—heavy, open, wood-hulled boats about twenty feet long, originally with sails, but later usually powered by outboards and steered with a long wooden tiller attached to a stern rudder.

One thing that kept Puakō alive was the availability of water here. Not only were there several anchialine ponds and two springs (near the church), but Hind had dug six wells during the development of the plantation. Two were still in use even recently, supplying brackish water to the Mauna Lani Resort for irrigation in their plant nursery behind Puakō. In the early days they provided just enough water for Hind to have alfalfa and guinea grass cultivated on some of the sugarcane land. Other commercial farming was tried in the Puakō area, and at one time or another corn, sweet potatoes, Hawaiian tobacco, cotton, mustard cabbage, tomatoes, coffee and watermelon were grown with varying rates of success, but no large-scale operations ever seemed to take root.

What the sources of water and feed did encourage was cattle ranching, and, while Hind never ran large herds in Puakō, the company did use the acreage as an area where they could fatten steers before shipping them to market from Kawaihae. Cattle were driven down from Puʻuwaʻawaʻa ranch and fed here for three or four months, usually during the summer. Puakō also became a welcome stop on cattle drives from ranches to the north. Steers from Kahuā Ranch, among others, would frequently rest and water for up to two weeks on their drives south toward Kona to find new pastures. The salt content of the Puakō water was a positive health factor for the animals, making it unnecessary to provide salt licks.

The Goto children worked gathering kiawe beans. These were either dried and shelled on the spot or ground, bagged and shipped by water to the Hind properties elsewhere. For this the children received 12½ cents for each 40-pound bag. At the time the mill closed, they had to walk a mile and a half from the shore to find kiawe. The predominant trees along the beach were curly koa, two varieties of sandalwood and hala. Behind the hala, except for the small kiawe woodland, open land stretched toward Mauna Kea. As the cattle and pigs fed on the kiawe, however, the seeds scattered in their droppings, rapidly enlarging the forest to the proportions we see today. This sudden growth of kiawe provided new sources of economic opportunity.

There was a large market for cooking firewood and charcoal to feed the domestic wood stoves in Honolulu. In about 1918, Ichiro Goto's journals report, "Yamada and Yamasota brought in a crew of Japanese workers", who spent two years in Puakō cutting kiawe and making charcoal. A sailing ship from Oʻahu called regularly. The wharf was improved to accommodate lighters that transported the products to the freighter.

Freighter Humuʻula *off Puakō, waiting for goods to be loaded, 1930s.*

As more modern stoves were developed, however, demand waned, and the operation closed down. Later the Fujii family moved from Paʻauilo to a house on the shore near Akona's, and Bunji Fujii made modest amounts of charcoal in two ovens (one near his house and another in the kiawe forest) well into the 1950s. Their house was destroyed in the tsunami of 1960, and they eventually bought property further down the road where Bunji's widow, Yusami, still resides part of the time. The charcoal production eventually devolved upon a man named Abe, who worked under contract to the Parker Ranch until recently.

Another opportunity was exploited by the Goto family, who started farming pigs, first for Hind and later for themselves. They allowed the pigs to run free and feed in the kiawe woods, and then trapped them for butchering or castration. Sometimes they cooked them for their customers. Ichiro Goto's journals have frequent entries of, "Kalua-ed [sic] a pig today." Visitors to Puakō frequently had to run the gauntlet of these animals, which were not noted for their amiability.

Baron Goto, the eldest Goto son, noted a favorite family pig story in his reminiscences. "One good friend [of my father] was a huge 250-pound Chinese-Hawaiian policeman—Akau. I may be wrong, but it appeared as though the duty of enforcing regulations against the making of home-brew was in the hands of federal officers. It evidently was not the responsibility of territorial policemen. Twice or sometime three times a year a federal agent used to visit the area and arrest those who were discovered with home-brew. Akau was usually

Ichiro Goto's pigs, 1940s.

forewarned of the visit and, when this happened, he promptly informed my father. My earliest recollection of Akau's activities was when I was about five years old. He came to call, as usual, on his horse. He talked to my father awhile. Soon my father brought a piece of rope and the two of them attached it to the barrel, which was sitting in the corner on the floor. A pole was passed through the loop and Akau helped father carry the barrel into the kiawe bush to hide it so that the federal agent would not find it.

"Akau left with a gallon of 'swipe' as a reward for informing father of the impending visit of the federal agent. It was a perfect set-up.

"A few days later, Akau came back to report to father that the inspector had come and gone. Akau had an empty gallon jug with him so father and he walked towards the area where the barrel was hidden. I followed them.

"As they approached the hiding place, they saw immediately that the barrel had been overturned and emptied. Nearby was a fat sow—flat on her side, snoring and dead drunk.... A rooster nearby was also quite wobbly. When he saw humans approaching, he attempted to walk away, but tumbled over. He spread his wings for better balance, tried to get up again, but could not quite make it, so he flopped over and gave up. Father, yelling terrible curses in Japanese, picked up the pole he had used to lift the barrel and struck the fat sow several times. But she was too drunk to feel the pain of the punishment. She merely grunted, turned over and went back to sleep.

"Akau thought this was all very funny, even though father did not. That day Akau did not have anything to put in his gallon jug."

The other, and more important, occupation of the Goto family was enlarging the kiawe honey operation that had started at the time of the sugar mill, and which they continued until the late 1960s. After 1924, the Goto family substantially increased production. Two Filipino workers, Lasaro and Santiago, were hired. They installed honey houses and hives from Waialea Bay on the north to Paniau on the south. They built frames, set foundations, harvested the honey, cut and strapped it and delivered it to the Puakō wharf in five-gallon cans for shipment to

Goto's Filipino employee and transportation, 1940s.

the United States and Europe on Swedish freighters, one of which was shipwrecked on the Puakō reef. In 1925, the Goto family was receiving seven to eight cents a pound for their product. During the Great Depression much of their market disappeared, but by 1939 they shipped 550 cases of honey, and by late 1941 they loaded 1000 containers, the peak of their production.

In 1953 the bees failed. There was disease in the kiawe and caterpillars destroyed the blossoms. Some of the desperate bees survived by eating their own honey, and reduced honey production

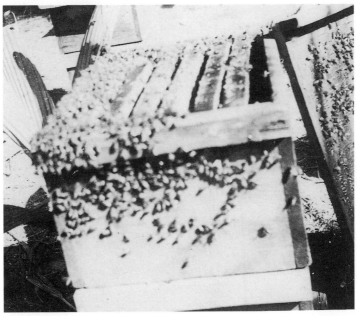

Goto's bees, late 1930s.

continued until a fire destroyed the last twenty-five hives in 1969.

Shipping Goto's honey from dock to Humuʻula, *late 1930s.*

Chapter VII

THREE
TRENDSETTING
NEWCOMERS
1929 to 1960

Kohala's most convivial fellow
The Marines arrive, and leave
Subdivision: lots of new lots

Life in Puakō might have gone on in this way almost forever had it not been for three people setting into motion events that paved the way for the eventual subdivision of the land. Oddly enough, none of the three—Leslie Wishard, Francis I'i Brown and Albert Ruddle—acquired land in Puakō proper, but by bracketing the area they created a setting for it, and it was only after being surrounded by gold that anyone noticed that Puakō was a gem.

Leslie Wishard bought two acres of land at Waialea Bay in 1929, later enlarging his holdings to twelve acres. He had the first frame house in the Puakō area built near the beach, a home that is still in use. Although it became a family vacation retreat, his wife and children lived there full-time for more than a year just after the house was completed. Katy, the younger daughter (now Mrs. John Lowrey), was frail, and the doctor felt the isolation would be healthier for her than the busy life of Kohala, where her father managed the family-owned Union Mill. At the beach they had a caretaker who cut kiawe for their stove with a machete that was also his chief weapon of defense against possible intruders, and the mother netted the fish that comprised a large part of their diet. On weekends, Wishard would come down from Māhukona by sampan bringing provisions, water and clean laundry. It was a primitive life, but definitely a healthy one and it produced warm and sometimes humorous memories. There were picnics at Puakō that were preceded by running the gauntlet of the Goto bees and the Goto pigs; there were shelling expeditions along the shore; there were brilliant warm nights when the children slept under an incandescent sky.

Soon after Wishard's purchase in Waialea, Francis Hyde Iʻi Brown acquired Kalāhuipuaʻa from Frank Woods, the widower of Eva Parker Woods. On this considerable property, given to

Eva by her father, Sam Parker, stood a small cottage and several ancient fishponds, all in disrepair, and not much else but black lava and white sand. It was the sort of challenge made to order for the new owner. Brown was the stuff of legend. Of Hawaiian royal blood, of great wealth and vast energy, he played championship golf and was regarded as perhaps the most convivial creature ever to inhabit the Kohala Coast.

A devoted lover of the land of Hawai'i, Brown threw himself into the development of his new domain with characteristic verve. He began by planting hundreds of coconut palms (with nuts from Leslie Wishard) in the thirties, cleaning and improving the fishponds with the help of Ichiro Goto and organizing a landing for his speedboat, the fastest on the island. Then (and continuing until he sold the property to Mauna Lani Resort in 1972) came the parties—formally organized or just seeming to happen, lasting sometimes for days or weeks, and including everyone from Hollywood celebrities to local fishermen, featuring boating expeditions, deep-sea fishing, bird shooting, pig hunting, fish netting in the ponds, swimming, diving, sunbathing, singing and dancing, everything accompanied by, always, incredible amounts of food and prodigious supplies of booze. Francis

Brown attracted people the way a magnet attracts iron filings, and soon he was serving as a one-man chamber of commerce for the Puakō area.

One of the persons he interested was Annabelle Dole Low Ruddle, who was looking for a quiet spot where she and her husband, Albert, and their four children could get away from rainy Hilo, where Albert owned a Ford agency. In 1937, she came

Landing at Paniau by boat. Ruddle family and friends.

down the coast by sampan, made a difficult landing on the wooded shore at Paniau and immediately fell in love. Hidden in the kiawe was an 'au 'au place, an ancient community bathing pool filled with brackish water and entered by stepping stones. She found a burial mound, old foundations from the original Puakō village and many splendid homesites on which to start anew. She returned to Hilo and convinced her husband to trade some Ruddle land in Hilo for seven and a half acres at Paniau. They had the property cleared and then built two houses near the shore and enlarged and improved the 'au 'au into a bona fide swimming and bathing pool. Everything for construction and sustenance was brought in by water. Two large metal rings were set in the lava onshore from a short channel where the boats secured a stern anchor. Supplies were either floated in or carried through the surf, according to their buoyancy.

Henry Doi at helm of sampan, bringing Ruddle family, friends and goods to Paniau, 1930s.

Family and visitors were known to arrive a little wet from their landing, which did not seem to deter a steady stream of relatives and friends who joined the Ruddle family at their compound.

In Puakō proper, there were a few new owners. Michael Kaloa had acquired land about halfway between the church and Paniau in 1925, property

Michael Kaloa, who purchased land at Waimā Point in 1920s.

that is still in the hands of one of his descendants, a member of the Laau family. The kuleana next to Jack Paulo's property passed eventually to Frank Rodrigues, who owned it until his death in 1938.

Michael Kaloa.

And there were a few more casual residents, Filipino fishermen who established a camp on the hill and plied their trade in "okole canoes", outriggers with outboard motors.

Party time at Paniau, 1940s. Clockwise beginning with man seated at bottom right: Junior Mann, Jewelle Lyman, Rachelle Kaʻaihili, Francis Lyman, Tita Ruddle (Spielman), Wally Young, Kekau Kawananakoa, Jack Ackerman, Claus Hayselden and Albert Kaʻaihili.

With World War II, Puakō became a little more accessible. The Marine Corps established a defense system overlooking Kawaihae harbor that consisted of paths, gun emplacements, bunkers, foxholes and an elaborate system of trenches. They also used the coast for invasion training. Landing sites were designated, and roads and trails were developed in the area south of Kawaihae. Among these improvements was a jeep track that wound along the shore as far as Kalāhuipua'a, crossing Paniau on the beach itself. While the Marines built a bridge just south of the present boat ramp that made it possible to bypass the kiawe forest, it still was necessary to wait for low tide to traverse the road between Spencer Beach and Mauna Kea Beach where no bridge had been added. Ichiro Goto patrolled this coastal road between Waialea Bay and Kalāhuipua'a for the Marines—usually on foot, but once in a while in his donkey wagon. When the war ended, the Marines sold much of their equipment, and the Ruddles, the Wishards

Jeep, acquired by Ruddle family after World War II.

Aerial view of Puakō, 1947, showing buildings

at Paniau and a stretch of beach.

and the Gotos, among others, acquired Jeep command cars. Now the trip to Doi's store in Kawaihae could be accomplished on land in a bone-rattling, kidney-jolting, two-hour drive.

In the late 1940s public interest in Puakō began to grow, and pressure was brought on the Territory to consider a subdivision. At first Francis Brown, then a territorial senator, fought the project. He was concerned that opening up the area would encourage casual visitors to his estate. Only after Annabelle Ruddle pointed out to him that the only land access to his property would be through hers and she promised to screen his callers did Brown become an enthusiastic supporter of a land sale. In fact, he contacted many of his circle of friends, urging them to buy land near his. Senators Brown, Silva and Awong, together with Leslie Wishard, formally petitioned the Territory to subdivide Puakō Beach. Thereafter, in 1950, a survey was made dividing the land into one hundred and sixty-three lots, to be laid out on either side of a road. Additional lots and another road were considered behind the shoreline development, but that idea was abandoned when it was ascertained that the water pressure was inadequate to support that large an area.

At the time of the land sale in 1952, Puakō was

Ichiro and Yukie Goto, 1940s.

not a very promising sight. Covered with kiawe forest right down to the beach, it was serviced by one water line and a single telephone line that was rather casually strung from Kawaihae. Electric power was not to come until 1957, when twenty owners bargained with the Hawaiian Electric Company to pay $20,000 to have a line brought in, with the proviso that they would be reimbursed if the service became profitable in three years— which it did. For access, there was still only the jeep trail along the shore, but a bulldozer was making a feeble stab at clearing what was desig- nated on the survey as "Puakō Beach Road", a forty-foot access that would reach almost to

Coral road through Puakō to Paniau, 1940s.

Paniau, where a note on the 1950 survey had stated, very optimistically, "end of paved road."

The land sale took the form of a public auction on the steps of the Territorial Offices in Hilo. To prevent speculation, no one was allowed to buy more than one lot (although married couples could buy two by putting one in the wife's name); a structure valued at a minimum of one thousand dollars was required on the property within five years. Bidding was to start at five hundred dollars for lots on the beach side and three hundred for those inland, and absentees could participate. Andy Morgan bought his property through a surrogate and then was not able to find its location in the forest for almost two years. Leon Thevenin, having accompanied Charles Murray when he surveyed the lots, knew which property he wanted, but he was bid up to almost seven hundred dollars by the competition. Families from the wet side of the island bought lots to use for weekend getaways. Frank De Luz bid in the auction and convinced relatives to buy property as well. Having purchased a beachfront lot at the sale, Frank then traded it for one across the street, because his wife didn't want to be too close to the water—a real-estate decision he was teased about for the rest of his life.

Bit by bit the new owners cleared their land

with the help of family, friends and Bunji Fujii, who was making charcoal from the kiawe harvest. One by one the houses were built, some from pre-fabricated kits, some from scratch and some from scrap. Although many were simple fishing shacks and none was luxurious by today's standards, an amazing number of them have survived until the present. Light still came from lanterns, water was still delivered preheated from the unburied single pipe and ice still came from Doi's store—a long, bumpy ride away. But the shoreline revealed by the clearing was breathtaking in its beauty, and the fishing, which had drawn the original Hawaiian settlers to our bay, was as good as ever. The water was warm and pellucid, and another generation of happy, tanned children learned to swim and fish in Puakō.

Despite all the new houses, the Fujii and Goto families continued to be almost the only full-time residents of Puakō until the late 1950s and early 1960s, although the Puakō Community Association was founded in 1958. Ed Austin provides a description of Puakō in 1959 when he and his wife, Mary, had occupied their newly constructed house for two months.

". . . There were a few others around. I think the . . . Mossman family moved to Puakō in 1957 or

1958. There was also a toothless character named Johnny Johnson, caretaker of the Guerrero residence at the south end of Puakō Road. At that time many Parker Ranch employees used Puakō for weekend fishing and boating, but they were not around weekdays. Only rarely did a car drive by—raising a cloud of dust—and we invariably, in our loneliness, strove to see who it was. Johnny Johnson, a consummate liar and teller of tall tales, was always preceded by a yapping dog, so when we saw our cat take to the trees, we knew we would shortly see Johnny. That gave us enough time to duck in from our outside shower and get some clothes on. Such was the society of Puakō circa 1960. . . ."

Chapter VIII

WE GET
MODERN

1960 to present

No more 'bumpty-bumpty road'
Destruction: account of a tsunami
1987 fire: overcoming big trouble

In the ensuing years, from 1960 to the present, Puakō has grown and coalesced into the community one sees today: a ribbon of houses along the winding shore, a thirty-eight unit condominium, two churches, a general store and an office complex. It has been a slow, evolutionary process.

In the early sixties, homeowners pressed for the paved road so lightly promised in the subdivision map. Fortunately for them, Judge Shunichi Kimura, soon to be elected first mayor of the island of Hawai'i, liked to spend leisure time away from the constant rains of Hilo. So several of our Puakō residents made it possible for him to use a house which was more than halfway down the beach road and which guaranteed him a liberal powdering of red dust each time he drove in. Not too much time elapsed before funds were allocated to improve and pave the Kawaihae-Puakō road. On January 10, 1964, the first segment was opened, and Ichiro Goto exulted, ". . . A beautiful one. No longer a bumpty-bumpty road. Perhaps if we live long enough there will be a road clear through to Kailua-Kona I guess."

Goto lived long enough, and the year 1975 found the Queen Ka'ahumanu Highway completed from the new Keāhole Airport to Kawaihae Harbor. For the first time it was possible to access this side of the island by car from the south. Formerly all vehicular traffic had come through Waimea. Mainland guests at the Mauna Kea Beach Hotel, which had opened in 1965, landed at the Hilo Airport and were driven over fifty miles to the resort. Now the whole western coastline opened up for discovery and development. In Puakō, our property values soared from around six hundred dollars a lot to as much as sixty thousand dollars. The first multi-family construction, the Puakō Beach Condominium, was completed the same year as the highway.

In 1966 the Hōkūloa Church was rededicated and a restoration drive inaugurated by the United

*Aerial view of Puakō, 1979, showing a stretch of waterfront
in Plat 4, with Waimā Point on the far right side.*

Note Queen Ka'ahumanu Highway near top of photo.

Aerial view of Puakō, 1990s, showing condominiums

and the store at left, and houses along the beach.

Church of Christ, the Episcopal Church in the
Hawaiian Islands and the Lutheran Mission
Council of Hawai'i. The goal was to reopen and
maintain the church and grounds for regular, ecumenical services. After years of neglect and disuse
and extensive damage by a tsunami in 1960, not
much was left but the outer walls, and it was estimated that $20,000 would be necessary to fund the
refurbishing. At this same time the building was
entered in the Registry of the National Trust for
Historic Preservation. The efforts at reconstruc-
tion, however, "fizzled" (as Annabelle Ruddle put

*Hōkūloa Church, Puakō, 1984. Credit: Hawaiian Mission
Children's Society Library, Mission Houses Museum.*

it), and, although partially useable, it was not until 1990 that the church was fully restored and rededicated under the auspices of the Hawaii Conference and Board of Homeland Ministries of the United Church of Christ. Over one thousand volunteer hours were donated to this cause, with The Reverend John Hoover as organizing minister.

At the same time that the 1966 effort was being launched for Hōkūloa, the Catholic Church was holding mass in Puakō in a grass shack under a coconut palm. Father Wilson Capodonna, a relief priest, led the congregation. A drive ensued to build a proper church; Laurence Rockefeller donated $10,000. S. K. Oda, a Hilo contractor, built the $135,000 structure, and the first permanently assigned priest, Father Joseph Mateis, sent out from Chicago, oversaw the construction. One of the early services in the new, modern Ascension Kalikonani church was a memorial in August 1978 for Bing Crosby, who had attended mass there when he was a guest at Mauna Kea Beach Hotel. Twelve singers from the resort staff sang "White Christmas", in a rendition that was as heartfelt as it was unseasonable. Over the years the church has enjoyed the support of mainland visitors as well as local parishioners.

If man has built during this period, nature has,

from time to time, destroyed. Life in Puakō has always engendered a healthy respect for the elements and vicissitudes of fate. From the earliest days, winds and wars and lava flows and storms and fires and tidal waves and droughts, epidemics and poverty have provided some of the glue that has held this village together. Uniting against adversity, it became a community. Surviving strengthened the bonds.

In 1960 our little settlement was struck by a tsunami, the by-product of an earthquake in Chile. The water height was recorded at nine feet in Kawaihae, the closest place where it was measured. Fortunately there was enough advance warning so that most residents were able to evacuate to the road to Waialea Bay. Although the Hapai house, just past Waimā Point, sailed out to sea and then back to shore (where it was deposited in its own fishpond), the major damage was confined to the area around the boat harbor, where six dwellings were destroyed and the church was gutted. The Fujii home was one of the casualties, and Bunji Fujii himself was rescued from a coconut palm after the waters receded.

Even more devastating was the 1946 tsunami, which Ichiro Goto described with great emotion in his journal. This eyewitness account was written the day after the event, and what follows is quoted exactly:

"The first wave came in at about 6:30 AM. After [it] hit these shores, everything was upset. The first wave reached about six feet around our home. I'd say it reached about to our bathhouse. The water started to recede slowly at first. Later it gained momentum and everything in its path was just sucked along with it.

"The receding action of the water looked as though it was against its will, moving slowly, stubbornly, but ever so strongly nothing can make it stop against that certain something which makes the wave move ever outward, away from land.

"The coral heads lifted their . . . shapes out of the ocean bottom like so many fantastic pictures. . . . I used to swim and spear fishes [here] in years passed. Now after looking [at] those bared coral shapes, they give me a sense of unreal weiredness [sic]. I'd never like to go amongst those beds of rock again.

"Puako Pt. as well as Ohai Pt. just stuck out like so many broken rock walls; the water spilling, cascading down the sides of the rocks looks like some little springs along Hamakua coast.

"I'd say most of the water just keeps on receding away from the land and . . . Puako Bay is empty for just a minute or two before another wave comes in like some unearthly monster. Roaring like a group of heavy bombers the wave comes in like some wild thing. Pushing rocks, fish, debri, everything and filling every space, and after the spaces are filled looks like some giant hand is pushing the wave up and above to a greater height; it again fills all spaces and comes roaring onto the land."

This tsunami was measured at twelve feet in Kawaihae, and coconut palms in Puakō had watermarks on their trunks as high as eight feet from the ground.

On January 8, 1980, the worst storm in living memory whipped across the island of Hawaiʻi. In Puakō, eighteen-foot waves broke over the reef, destroying over half the underwater coral, pounding into seawalls and crashing onto the shore. At one point, at the height of the gale, a huge, wave-driven coconut log pummeled the shoreline from south to north, acting like a battering ram on anything in its path. Our village was evacuated for a time, and when the residents returned they found three houses destroyed and eighty-three damaged by sea water that had flooded over the road.

Probably the most defining disaster in Puakō's recent history was the fire of 1987. It was not the first to strike this area. A son of Lorenzo Lyons described a fire in the mid 1800s that burned from Mauna Loa to Mauna Kea and down the hills to Puakō, and in the early years of this century underground fires were known to burn for months behind the sugar plantation. The cane workers used mules and a plow to create firebreaks and protect the community. In 1977, a fire in Waialea Bay destroyed the Leslie Wishard, Jr. home, damaged two others and was mercifully stopped at the boat ramp after burning over one hundred acres of brush and kiawe.

But nothing that had occurred heretofore could have prepared our residents for the horror of 1987 that began on Wednesday, July 1, with a clear dawn and a light wind that picked up in the afternoon as people noticed smoke rising to the north. Campers on the state land behind Waialea Bay had lit a campfire, which was caught by the rising wind—that good old Puakō ʻŌlauniu, dust-raising, mischief-making wind—and quickly spread out of control. The flames coursed down the hill toward the houses around the bay, but the response of neighbors who grabbed garden hoses, wet down roofs and put out spot fires, plus the arrival of two fire trucks, made it appear initially that the blaze would be controlled. But steadily increasing winds drove the flames several hundred feet downwind toward the Puakō dump, where they jumped the road. Then people realized the gravity of the situation. By that time, the wind was gusting up to forty-five miles an hour.

Ed Austin, by this time a permanent resident, described the rest of the afternoon: " I . . . took another ride back toward the dump but quickly saw flames on both sides of the road. . . . We were in big trouble! We hurried home knowing we would have to flee but believing we would have to leave everything behind and leave on foot through the Ruddles. . . . I told Mary to pack our most precious possessions and close up the house while I scurried around locating valuable records. Then Joe Mossman [who was chief of the volunteer fire department] came by speaking through a bullhorn telling us to evacuate immediately. From this we assumed we could get the car out. . . . As we got near the condo we had to turn our lights on as the smoke and fire were so bad. The firemen directed us around their trucks. Fire raged on both sides of the road, especially so near the boat ramp. We just kept going and soon were at the dump and out of it. Evacuees were beginning to park all along the road and highway watching the fire tear into the woods behind Puakō. We thought for sure our homes were doomed as we did much of the next two days as smoke and fire continued to rage through the woods."

Most of the local firefighting equipment was already involved dealing with a 500-acre blaze at Puʻuanahulu, but volunteers from Puakō, Waikoloa and Kohala augmented the available units until additional help arrived at Puakō. Eventually the response included men and equipment from seven fire stations, county and state workers, military and forestry personnel, civil defense, police, the Red Cross and private citizens. Four tanker trucks and the county helicopter were involved; bulldozers and operators from five private companies cleared firebreaks, and over a thousand feet of hoses were deployed by firefighters.

Leilani Hino, a reporter for *West Hawaii Today* who was living here at the time, described the scene on Thursday, July 2:

"The firemen had been patrolling up and down the stretch of Puako Beach Drive all night and all day, focusing on spots where the fire looked like it might threaten homes. They moved back and forth from area to area, constantly protecting one house or another.

"When Chief Smith got an urgent call to a structure burning on the mauka side of Puako Beach

Drive, he indicated I could ride along with him. As we reached the scene of the burning house a helicopter was dumping bucketloads of water on it. The wind had shifted and driven the fire into the tiny beach house without warning. Firemen played streams of water on the small structure, but it went like a tinderbox. In minutes the house was gone.

"Down towards the end of the road where the petroglyph field lies, the wind was playing havoc ... driving the flames toward a lone man standing on his roof with a garden hose. The firemen rushed to his aid."

By Friday, the fire was controlled, although not completely extinguished. The winds, which had gusted to fifty-five miles per hour the day before, had subsided and damage assessment began. Four houses in Waialea Bay and three in Puakō had been totally destroyed, and there was more than a million dollars in property loss. While the total destruction of homes in Puakō was confined to the mauka side of the road, several roofs were lost on the makai side, and along one stretch most of the trees caught fire from wind-driven embers. Many of the surviving homes, like the Stevenson residence, had considerable water damage, and everyone suffered from the smoke and soot. On the other hand, over two hundred homes valued at over twenty million dollars had been saved, and, although twelve firefighters had been treated for smoke inhalation and minor burns, there were no serious injuries and no loss of life.

Leilani returned to Puakō late Friday just as residents were being allowed to return to their homes. "A long line of cars wound slowly down Puako Beach Drive, passing through the roadblock at the dump. Blackened kiawe trees, uprooted by bulldozers, lay grotesquely in the smoldering ashes . . . a wide firebreak had been cut around the Puako condominiums. Behind every house where there had been dense kiawe forest there was now burned out desolation. The line of cars thinned as they peeled off one-by-one into driveways on both sides of the road.

"I turned into my driveway and was amazed to see that everything looked perfectly normal in the front yard. I noticed that the hose I had at the front of the house had been moved to a spigot at the back of the house. I walked around to the back yard and found the mango and breadfruit trees in good shape, with hardly any damage at all. Someone must have sprayed a lot of water out there when the fire passed."

Leilani was not the only beneficiary of

neighborly help. All over Puakō and Waialea Bay, people had responded to the emergency with out-pourings of aid. Neighbors who put out spot fires saved most of the homes in Waialea Bay until the arrival of the fire trucks. When a coconut palm near Ed Austin's house burst into flame, his neighbor, Peter Merriman, ran across the street, grabbed a garden hose and saved both the palm and the house. Frank Hammerslage, a Waikoloa volunteer, climbed up on a burning roof with water and saved the Bracher residence.

For days, fire departments kept a presence in the community as they continued to monitor small fires and wet down the trees and roadway while homeowners worked side by side with them putting Puakō back together again. Our residents showed their gratitude in many ways. Some took out thank-you advertisements in the newspaper; some wrote letters of appreciation to the fire depart-ment and to the police; and one of the firemen from Waimea, Tom Beach, still remembers the individual homeowners who shared one of the few things they had to offer: "People kept giving us these wonder-ful, juicy mangoes."

After the fire, when everyone was home again and picking up the pieces, there were various re-ports that the marching men had been heard on dark, windy nights. No one ever saw them, so no one has ever been certain whether they were warriors or a makahiki procession or an ancient celebration or just a few old neighbors dropping by to see how things were coming along.

 # GLOSSARY

ahupua'a. Land division, usually from the uplands to the sea.

Akahi. One of the Hawaiian families that claimed Puakō land under the Mahele.

Akau. A Hawaiian family that has lived in Kawaihae for generations.

Akona. The Hawaiian family that built a stone house on the original Akahi property.

Ali'i. Chief. To rule or act as a chief.

Aloha. An affectionate greeting, used as hello, goodbye or farewell.

'Anaeho'omalu. Bay, well known for petroglyphs, in South Kohala District.

anchialine ponds. Small bodies of water unique to leeward Hawai'i consisting of a mix of fresh and salt waters that rise and fall with the tides yet have no direct, visible connection with the ocean.

'au 'au. A bath house or bathing pool.

Auwae. A Hawaiian family of Kahunas that lived and practised in Puakō.

'Auwai. Irrigation ditches.

Hakau. An ancient chief of Waipi'o.

Hala'ula. An area in the North Kohala district.

hale. A small house.

Hale-o-Kapuni. A heiau site near Kawaihae where sharks were fed.

Hāmākua. A district in the northeast portion of the Island of Hawai'i.

haole. A white person or foreigner.

Hapai. An early family in Puakō.

Hāpuna. The bay and land division immediately north of Puakō.

hau. A lowland tree with heart-shaped leaves and yellow flowers.

Hawai'i. The largest island in the Hawaiian group.

Hāwī. A village and land division in the North Kohala district.

Heau. Shrubs or trees of the sandalwood family.

he'e. Octopus.

Heiau. A pre-Christian high place of Hawaiian worship; a shrine.

Hō'ea. The location of a sugar mill in the North Kohala district.

Hōkūloa. The evening star; the name given by Lorenzo Lyons to the church in Puakō in 1860.

Honoka'a. A town in the Hāmākua district.

Honolulu. The capital of the State of Hawai'i, situated on the island of O'ahu.

Hukia/Hukia'a. Land in the North Kohala district.

'iliahi. Hawaiian sandalwood.

Ka'ahumanu. The favorite wife of Kamehameha; his queen.

Ka'eo. The name of a trail.

Kāhili. A symbol of Hawaiian royalty consisting of an elaborate feather standard atop a long pole which was carried by a high noble of the court.

Kaho'olawe. An uninhabited island near Maui.

Kahuā. A ranch in the North Kohala district.

Kahuna. A priest, minister, sorcerer or expert in any profession.

Kaiana. A famous warrior and lieutenant of Kamehameha I.

Kailua. Village and ancient surfing area, Kona district of Hawai'i.

Kalāhuipua'a. The land division immediately south of Puakō; sold by Francis I'i Brown to Mauna Lani Resort.

Kalaniopu'u. The uncle of Kamehameha I and son of Keawe; chief at the time of Captain Cook.

Kamalālāwalu. A Maui chief who was defeated in battle on the plains behind Puakō.

Kanaloakuaana. A chief who battled Kamalālāwalu on the plains behind Puakō; guardian of his younger brother, Lonoikamakahiki.

kapu. A taboo or prohibition.

Ka'ūpūlehu. A land division near the sea in the North Kona District.

Kawaihae. A harbor and former fishing and trading village north of Puakō.

konohiki. The headman of an ahupua'a.

Lālāmilo. In legend, the husband of Puakō. Now the land division of Puakō.

lehua. The flower of the 'ōhi'a tree; also the tree.

Lono. One of the four major Hawaiian gods.

Lonoikamakahiki. A chief who battled Kamalālāwalu on the plains behind Puakō.

loulu. A short native fan palm.

Lunalilo. A Hawaiian king who died in 1874 and who owned a large plot of land in Puakō near the site of the condominium.

Mahele. The land division of 1848, known as "The Great Mahele", in which western methods of land recording and ownership were applied to the Hawaiian Islands.

Mahikihia Heiau. A burial heiau near the present Mauna Kea Beach Hotel.

Māhukona. A land section and harbor in the North Kohala district.

Mailekini. An ancient heiau immediately below Pu'ukoholā near Kawaihae.

Mailelauli'i. One of five sisters from Kona who fell in love with the saltmaker, Puakō.

Makahiki. An annual harvest festival in ancient Hawai'i which was also an occasion for tax collection.

makai. Toward the water. Used as a term of direction and location.

Makua Laiana. The Hawaiians' name for Rev. Lorenzo Lyons (1807–1886), meaning "Father Lyons."

Manuwai. The nickname, meaning "seabird", for Wilmot Vredenberg, manager of the Puakō Sugar Plantation.

Maui. Second-largest island in the Hawaiian group, named for the demi-god Māui.

mauka. Toward the mountains or inland. Used as a term of direction and location.

Moloka'i. An island in the Hawaiian group.

mua. A men's eating house in ancient Hawaiian culture.

Ne'ula. The mother of Lālāmilo, who lived upland from Puakō.

O'ahu. The most populous island in the Hawaiian group and the seat of government.

'Ōhai Point. A point of land in Puakō Bay.

'ōhi'a. A native tree, sometimes called lehua.

'Ōlauniu. The name of a promiscuous local wind on Hawai'i.

Pa'auilo. A village in the Hāmākua district.

Pahauna Heiau. A heiau built on the hill near the entrance to Puakō that was a shrine to healing.

Pai. A family that lived in the Puakō area.

pandanus. A type of palm used for weaving and thatching.

Paniau. The area at the south end of Puakō.

Paulo, Jack. An early Puakō resident and guardian of local Hawaiian lore.

Pauoa Bay. A bay at the southern end of Puakō.

Pele. The legendary volcano goddess who lives on the island of Hawai'i.

Pelikane. A sentinel stone of the Pahauna heiau; Englishman in Hawaiian.

piko. Umbilical cord.

pili. A native grass often used for thatching in Hawai'i.

Pouhala. The valley on O'ahu where the Puakō locomotive was abandoned.

Puakō. A village, bay and point in the South Kohala district of Hawai'i; the tassel of the sugar cane; the name of a princess from Puna who married Lālāmilo; the name of a poor saltmaker.

Puna. A district in the southeast portion of the island of Hawai'i.

Pupualenalena. A thieving dog mentioned in ancient Hawaiian legends and tales.

Pu'uanahulu. A hill and land section near Puakō.

Pu'uepa. A land division in the North Kohala district.

Puʻukoholā. A heiau near Kawaihae, constructed by Kamehameha I. A national historic site.

Puʻuloa. A land section at the south end of the island of Hawaiʻi.

Puʻuwaʻawaʻa. Land division and peak in the North Kona district of Hawaiʻi.

supercargo. An officer on a merchant ship in charge of the commercial concerns of the voyage. (In this case, Vredenberg was in charge of shepherding Portuguese immigrants.)

tsunami (Japanese). A great sea wave produced by submarine earth movement or volcanic eruption.

Uli. A heiau near Waimea restored by Kamehameha I.

Waialea. A bay between Hāpuna and Puakō, locally known as Beach 69.

Waikoloa. A land section in the South Kohala district of Hawaiʻi.

Waimā. A point of land in Puakō.

Waimea. A village in the South Kohala district of Hawaiʻi at 3,000 feet. Headquarters of the Parker Ranch.

Waipiʻo. A valley and ancient surfing place in the Hāmākua district of the island of Hawaiʻi.

BIBLIOGRAPHY

BOOKS

A Proposal for the Establishment of the William Ellis Trail, Honolulu, Friends of the William Ellis Trail, 1974, 28 pp.

Atlas of Hawaii, 2nd ed., Honolulu, The University of Hawaii Press, 1983, 238 pp.

A Voyage of Discovery—in the Years 1790, 91, 92, 93, 94 and 1795 in Discovery and Chatham Under Command of Capt. George Vancouver, London, 1798, 3 vols.

A Voyage of Discovery into the South Sea and Bering's Straits on the Ship Rurich under the Command of Otto Von Kotzebue, London, 1821, 3 vols.

Beaglehole, J. C., *The Life of Captain James Cook,* Stanford, Stanford University Press, 1974, 760 pp.

Bird, Isabella, *Six Months in the Sandwich Islands,* Honolulu, University of Hawaii Press, 1966, 278 pp.

Buck, Peter, *Vikings of the Pacific,* 5th imprint, Chicago, University of Chicago Press, 1972, 339 pp.

Cox, J. Halley with Stasack, Edward, *Hawaiian Petroglyphs,* 6th printing, Honolulu, Bishop Museum Press, 1990, 100 pp.

Craighill, E. S. and Handy, Elizabeth Green, *Native Planters in Old Hawaii,* Honolulu, Bishop Museum Press, 1972, 676 pp.

Daws, Gavan, *Shoal of Time,* Honolulu, University of Hawaii Press, 1968, 493 pp.

De Freycinet, Louis Claude de Saulses, *Hawaii in 1819: a Narrative Account,* translated by Ella L. Wiswell, Pacific Anthropological Records No. 26, Honolulu, Bishop Museum, 1978, 138 pp.

Department of Anthropology, *Report on a Walk-Through Archeological Survey of the Puakō Beach Lots Spur Road Alignment, Lalamilo, South Kohala, Hawaii Island,* Honolulu, Bishop Museum, 1972, 5 pp.

Doyle, Emma Lyons, *Makua Laiana: The Story of Lorenzo Lyons,* Honolulu, Honolulu Star Bulletin, 1945, 259 pp.

Ellis, William, *Polynesian Researches*, new edition, Rutland, Vt., Charles E. Tuttle Company, 1969, 414 pp.

Ellis, William, *The Journal of William Ellis,* Rutland, Vt., Charles E. Tuttle Company, 1979, 363 pp.

Environmental Assessment, Mauna Kea Properties Queen's Lands Golf Course, Honolulu, Belt Collins & Associates, 1991.

Fitzpatrick, Gary L., *The Early Mapping of Hawaii, vol. I,* Honolulu, Editions Limited, 1986, 160 pp.

Fornander, Abraham, *Hawaiian Antiquities and Folk-lore,* reprint from Bishop Museum Press, Millwood, New York, Kraus Reprint, 1985, 6 vols.

Foster, Nelson, *Bishop Museum and the Changing World of Hawaii,* Honolulu, Bishop Museum Press, 1993, 95 pp.

Goldsberry, Stephen, *Maui, the Demigod,* Honolulu, University of Hawaii Press, 1989, 410 pp.

Grant, Glen, *Hawaii, the Big Island,* Honolulu, Mutual Publishing Company, 1988, 240 pp.

Harrison Associates, *Draft Environmental Impact*

Statement, Hapuna Beach State Recreation Area Expansion, Honolulu, Division of State Parks, 1996, pp not numbered.

Hind, John, ed. R. Renton Hind, *John Hind of Hawi,* available as a photocopy fragment.

Illustrated Atlas of Hawaii, edited by O. A. Bushnell, 15th printing, Honolulu, Island Heritage Publishing, 1991, 71 pp.

Johnson, Dorothy O. and Small, Dana, eds., *Voyage of the Columbia Around the World with John Boit, 1790– 1793,* Portland, Oregon, Beaver Books, 1960.

Kalakaua, King David, *Legends and Myths of Hawaii,* edited by Hon. R. M. Daggett, Rutland, Vt., Charles E. Tuttle Company, 1972, 530 pp.

Kamakau, Samuel M., *Ruling Chiefs of Hawaii,* rev. ed., Honolulu, The Kamehameha School Press, 1992, 512 pp.

Kirch, Patrick Vinton, *Archeological Reconnaissance Survey of Kalahuipua'a and portions of Waikoloa, Lalamilo, and Anaeho'omalu, South Kohala, Hawaii Island,* Honolulu, Bishop Museum, 1973, 90 pp.

Kirch, Patrick Vinton, *Marine Exploitation in Prehistoric Hawaii, Archeological Investigations at Kalahuipua'a, Hawaii Island,* Pacific Anthropological Records No. 29, Honolulu, Bishop Museum, 1979, 235 pp.

Ledyard, John, *Journal of Capt Cook's Last Voyage to the Pacific Ocean,* 1783.

Lisianski, Urey, *A Voyage Round the World in the Years 1803, 4, 5, & 6, Performed by the Order of his Imperial Majesty, Alexander the First, Emperor of Russia, in the Ship Neva,* London, 1814.

Martin, Lynn J., ed., *Na Paniola o Hawaii,* Honolulu, State Foundation of Culture and the Arts, no date, 99 pp.

Meares, John, *Voyages Made in the Years 1788 and 1789, with an Introductory Narrative of a Voyage Performed in the year 1786, from Bengal, in the Ship Nootka,* London, 1791.

Neal, Marie C., *In Gardens of Hawaii,* Honolulu, Bishop Museum, 1965, 924 pp.

Piercy, LaRue W., *Hawaii Island Leaders,* published by the author, 44 pp.

Piercy, LaRue W., *Big Island History Makers,* Honolulu, Mutual Publishing, 1990, 44 pp.

Pukui, Mary Kawena and others, *New Pocket Hawaiian Dictionary,* Honolulu, University of Hawaii Press, 1992, 257 pp.

Pukui, Mary Kawena and others, *Place Names of Hawaii,* revised edition, Honolulu, University of Hawaii Press, 1974, 289 pp.

Smart, Colin D., *A Report of Excavations on Site H22, Puakō, Hawaii Island,* Honolulu, Bishop Museum, 1964, 16 pp.

Soil Survey of the Island of Hawaii, U.S. Department of Agriculture, Soil Conservation Service, 1973.

Spoehr, Anne Harding, *The Royal Lineages of Hawai'i,* Honolulu, Bishop Museum Press, 1989, 22 pp.

Stokes, John F. G., *Heiau of the Island of Hawai'i,* Honolulu, Bishop Museum Press, 1991, 196 pp.

The Hawaii Book, Chicago, J. G. Ferguson Publishing Company, 1961, 336 pp.

Thomas, Mifflin, *Schooner from Windward,* Honolulu, University of Hawaii Press, 1983.

Tomonari-Tuggle, M. J., *An Archeological Reconnaissance Survey of a Parcel Adjoining the Puakō Petroglyph Fields,* Prepared for the Waimea Hawaiian Civic Club and Mauna Lani Resort, 7 pp.

Tregaskis, Richard, *The Warrior King,* Honolulu, Falmouth Press, 1973, 320 pp.

Welch, David J., *Archeological Reconnaissance of the Area South of the Puakō Petroglyph Archeological District, South Kohala, Hawaii,* Honolulu, Bishop Museum, 1984, 16 pp.

BIBLIOGRAPHY
ARTICLES

Apple, Russell A., "Pahukanilua: Homestead of John Young", Historical Data Section of the Historic Structure Report, National Park Service, typescript, 90 pp.

Austin, Ed, "Early Days", typescript.

Baker, Albert S., Hawaiian Annual for 1919—More Petroglyphs (Pu'uanalulu and Honolkohau).

Bates, George Washington, Sandwich Islands Notes by a Haole, New York, 1854.

Bennett, C. C., Honolulu Directory and Historical Sketch of the Hawaiian or Sandwich Islands, Honolulu, 1869.

"Ciguratera, Fish Poisoning", Hawai'i Department of Health.

Cleveland, Richard J., "A Narrative of Voyages and Commercial Enterprises", Cambridge, 1842.

Duefrene, Pat, "View into the Past: Mauna Lani Resort, Hawai'i", Mauna Lani Resort, 1991, foldover.

Ednie, Sandra, "Puakō, Hawaii", typescript, 8 pp.

Ellis, William and others, "Journal of a Tour around Hawaii by a Deputation from the Mission of Those Islands", Boston, 1825.

Emerson, N. B., "Pele and Hiiaka, a Myth from Hawaii", *Sandwich Island Gazette*, 1836.

"Enjoy the Living Sea", University of Hawaii Sea Grant Extension Service.

Fornander, Abraham, *Sandwich Islands Monthly Magazine,* 1956.

Godfrey, Pat, "Makua Laiana", *The Waimea Gazette* (December, 1987): 14–15.

Goto, Baron, "The Other Side of the Canefield", typescript.

Goto, Ichiro, "Journals", handwritten documents.

Grove, Noel, "Volcanoes, Crucibles of Creation", *National Geographic Magazine* (December, 1992) Vol. 182, No. 6: 5–41.

"Hawaiian Sea Turtles", National Marine Fisheries Service and Center for Marine Conservation, Mauna Lani Resort, Inc. and University of Hawaii Sea Grant Extension Service, 1991.

Hendricks, Pete, "Kawaihae, Birth of a Kingdom", *The Waimea Gazette* (March, 1992): 6–7.

Hall, Jack, "Kohala's Gay Nineties or the Log of the Luna", typescript circa 1915.

Hino, Leilani, *West Hawaii Today*, July 2, 1987.

Kennedy, J., "Archeology of Paniau", Sept. 1980, publication unknown.

"Kohala", *Sunset, the Magazine of Western Living* (November, 1966): 64–70.

Melrose, Maile, "Petroglyphs . . . a Walk Through Time", *The Waimea Gazette* (March, 1992): 10–12.

"Preservation News Briefs", *Historic Hawai'i* (June, 1991): 10.

"Recreational and Weather Guide", Hawaii the Big Island, University of Hawaii Sea Grant Program.

Rivas, Carlos, "Au apa'apa'a—Passing of Much Time on

One Piece of Land by an Old Family", *The Waimea Gazette* (September, 1992): 14–19.

"The Climate System", *Reports to the Nation* (1991), UCAR and NOAA.

Waimea Report (1833, 1839, 1841, 1846, 1851, 1857, 1858, 1859, 1860, 1862, 1863), Records in the Hawaiian Mission Children's Society Library.

ILLUSTRATIONS

ALOHA...